All Write
How to Start, Structure, and Sustain a Writing Group

DEBORAH L. MANDEL

UNCOPYEDITED EDITION

Not for resale; do not quote from this edition.

https://www.chrysaliscopyediting.com/

debbielmandel@gmail.com

This book is dedicated to Jim,
my inspiration.

And to Claire, Dianne, and Mary of
Shoreline Writers, without whom my words would
be empty and my thoughts unexpressed.
You have inspired me, motivated me, and held
me accountable every word of the way.

Table of Contents

Acknowledgements

I owe a debt of gratitude to Dianne Hearn, Mary Reynolds, and Claire Smith, my Shoreline Writers group, without whom this book would not be. Together, we created a process that worked so well I was moved to share it with the world. They are part of every word written here. To the three of you, thank you is not enough.

Many thanks to Maureen Shortt, Jessica Ellis, Daphne Nielsen, Carol Bozena, and Darlene Dunbar, my first readers, who gave me honest feedback and helped me take the next steps to make this book accessible, readable, and understandable for everyone interested in being part of a writing group.

Much appreciation goes to Liza Mandel, my sister, for her eagle eye in editing the manuscript and pointing out ways to clarify the sections that might have been just a wee bit obtuse.

Thank you to Mette Harrison for graciously sharing her writing expertise with my readers.

And finally, to my husband, Jim Benn, the best writing mentor a person could have. Your inspiration, encouragement, and unwavering support are the bedrock upon which this book took form. I'll run with you forever.

Introduction

Shortly after retiring, I attended a writing course. I finally had the time to pursue a desire I'd had for many years—to write a novel. In that class, I met three other women who were interested, as was I, in forming a writing group to support one another in our endeavors to write and publish. Shoreline Writers was established. Several books have been written, several more are almost done. *All Write*, which has been two years in the making, is finished! Shoreline Writers was the inspiration for this book, and without my group's support and excellent critiquing, this would not be in readers' hands today.

All Write is Shoreline Writers' story. Using our group as an example, I hope to inspire you on your journey to form a writing group of your own and write that story that needs to be told.

The basic guidelines presented here for how a group works are applicable to everyone. The specifics of those guidelines are not. Take for example the importance of time. Three of us, when we formed Shoreline Writers, were retired. The fourth woman, a mother of three, was between jobs. We all had A LOT of time on our hands, so when you read about the number of hours we spent writing and editing each week, don't panic! We could do that. You might not have the luxury of so much free time. You may be a parent, or working, or working and a parent, or, even harder—a single parent and working.

I remember those times well. For five years, I was a single mom with two young boys, working, and going to college. There was NO time. But my desire to earn a degree was strong enough to overcome the many hurdles I faced along the way. That is also true of writing. If you have the passion, the hurdles are surmountable. I remember an author at a writing conference talking about how she wrote her first book holding an infant, and then toddler, on her lap for two hours early every morning. It was the only way she could write, and she had to write. Maybe you're in the sandwich generation and taking care of parents as well as children. Some of you may be older and less computer savvy. Others of you might be younger and think you have nothing to write about. If it's your dream, give it your best shot.

I want to support you in joining a writing group which will in turn support you in your writing. All of you. Regardless of your other time commitments. I designed this book to be accessible to everyone. Create a group with other individuals who are in similar life situations; a group that can support you in whatever your life circumstances currently are. Maybe you can only meet every other week. Okay. Maybe you can only meet monthly. Okay. Twice a year? That's fine. Being retired gave the three of us a luxury of time that we deeply appreciated. When the between-jobs mom became a working mom, she had a lot of balls in the air. The group supported her with that, and she maintained a strong commitment to the group. What I will reinforce over and over in *All Write* is that it is the commitment you make to the group that supports you in your process and helps you with your writing. The frequency of how often a group meets is arbitrary; your commitment to the group is crucial.

In this book, I have included exercises which we used during meetings to help us build our group and hone our writing skills. But please remember, five years of our meetings have been condensed into less than 150 pages. Which means there is a lot of material covered in these pages that took us years to develop. So again, don't panic. This is not a book to read at one sitting. This is a guide to use over time as you and your group evolve. We would spend weeks to months in weekly meetings working on voice, or tense, or point of view. I don't expect you to read the book, do each exercise once, and *presto!* you understand it all. There is a learning curve.

Writing is hard work. Learning the ins and outs of writing is hard work. Doing the exercises I have provided is hard work. You could certainly skip all this and write on your own. Many, many writers are successful without a group. But being in a group helps to carry you through the hard work to produce the kind of story that you want. The group offers support, motivation, holds you accountable, holds your hand, encourages you, teaches you, and gives you a team of comrades who know exactly what you are going through, as they either have gone or are going through the same growing pains.

That is the joy of a group.

Debbie Mandel

PART ONE

How to Create a Successful Writing Group

Do you have a book in you waiting to be written? Perhaps it's a memoir about your favorite great-uncle or a summer camp experience at age ten that shaped your life. Or it's a travel journal based on your exploration of Southeast Asia. Maybe it's a how-to book about how to paint with oils or how to create sculptures from scrapyard materials.

Do *you* have a story to tell?

How many times have you thought, *Wow, that would be a great first line for a book?* How many times have you said to yourself *I could have done a better job writing that story?* How many times have you wondered if you had it in you to sit down and finish a book? *How many years* have you mulled over a storyline in your head while thinking, *If only I had the time, or the support, or the know-how?*

If any of these scenarios sound familiar, then *All Write* can help you create a writers' group to support you in your process.

CHAPTER ONE
It Takes a Group

Find a group of people who challenge and inspire you;
spend a lot of time with them, and it will change your life.
—Amy Poehler

Shoreline Writers was created in 2015 by four women who met in a writing class at a local Connecticut university. When the six-week course was finished, we weren't. One woman had written the first draft of a semi-autobiographical work of fiction. (It is common that everyone's first book is at least semi-autobiographical.) The second woman was writing a book for her daughters about their great-great-grandmother. The third woman wasn't writing anything but had just retired and was ready to start her great American novel. The fourth woman (she left the group within the first year) was writing a memoir.

We were a varied group of wannabe writers who had three things in common: We wanted to write. We wanted support in that process. And we wanted to talk about our writing. Just as having a running buddy will get you out on the road every morning at the crack of dawn when you'd much rather be sleeping, a writing group provides motivation by holding you accountable in the writing process. We have found both the motivation and accountability to be invaluable.

Let's hear from our members about why they wanted to join a group.

MARY: I'd grown up with the image of a solitary writer sequestered in a room, hunched over a typewriter, pecking away on a masterpiece. So when I retired and decided to write a memoir, I followed that model. I holed up in my studio over the garage, until I'd churned out a true-life novel, loosely based on my mother's life. Friends and family edited the first and second drafts with tremendous encouragement. I thought

I had a winner! My husband, the sensible one, recommended I attend a six-week writing course at a local university prior to pushing the *go button* and submitting my manuscript to agents.

The course on fiction and memoir writing was perfect. My classmates shared stories that left me laughing, crying, and clutching my heart. The feedback sessions opened my eyes. I knew I had a crackerjack story, but by the middle of the course, I was having serious doubts about my manuscript. I'd broken most of Stephen King's rules for aspiring writers. I had too much tell and not enough show, and I'd paved the way to hell with adverbs. I knew if I was going to succeed as an author, I needed to be surrounded by a community of peers and not work as a solitary writer.

DIANNE: I have fancied myself a potential writer since my ninth grade English teacher accused me of plagiarizing Jack London. Decades later, I tested my perception of self by taking a writing class. It was humbling; I had a lot to learn! On the final day of class, I was approached to join a writing group. I'd never heard of such a thing, but instinctively felt it was right. We were a compatible collection of four writers-in-the-making. We made progress and developed our voices, but the group disbanded for a number of convivial reasons. Several years later, a member of the original writing group invited me to join her new writing group. I knew I had a book to write, so I was grateful for the opportunity.

CLAIRE: After spending over a decade of arrogantly telling relatives that I would write the story of our great-grandmother, I realized that for some reason, I did not do it. I wanted to. I started it. I would buckle down for a few days, then let it go again. So my main reason for joining a writing group was to stop this pattern. Accountability with deadlines had worked for me in my career, so I thought it would cure this procrastination.

And—I'm so embarrassed to admit this now—the thought of having others rave about my story, which I was certain was the best plot ever written, and compliment my writing, which I was certain was flawless, was appealing.

DEBBIE: I've always wanted to write a novel. When I retired in 2015, I no longer had the excuse of not enough time. If I was going to write a book it was now or never. I signed up for a writing course, and when several students talked about starting a writing group at the conclusion of the class, I signed up for that as well.

I had been in a writing group several years before and treasured the support I received. At that time, I was writing a nonfiction book about my work as a psychotherapist. None of us had written a book before, nor did we really know what we were doing, but we muddled through. One woman was scripting a sci-fi play. Another woman was creating a children's book. A third woman was writing a memoir about her mother, then changed direction entirely to focus on creating an electronic newsletter about local events. (She became a successful e-writer with this idea.) But this group was loosely organized. We took turns reading our work and giving feedback, most of which consisted of our being too nice to one another, piling on the encouragement, and shying away from tough critiquing. We never became skilled at the art of editing.

I wanted to recreate that experience, but with a more knowledgeable group of writers, with more expertise. Shoreline Writers has motivated me in an entirely different way than my first group. They are a collection of serious writers committed to getting their books finished. They are inspiring, and I haven't regretted a moment of it.

If you would like to learn how to create a writers' group to support you in the writing process, *All Write* is the book for you. It doesn't matter if you write fiction or nonfiction, sci-fi or historical fiction, memoir or biography, young adult or adult. Maybe you haven't written before, maybe you have. Maybe you've thought about it for ten years, maybe it's a new passion. Maybe you want to write for yourself or your family, maybe you want to get published, mainstream or self-published. None of that matters. Whatever your reasons are for wanting to write, honor that desire. I have written this book because I was thrilled with what we'd created at Shoreline Writers, and I wanted to share what I'd learned with you.

Write What You Know

This bit of writing wisdom is attributed to both Ernest Hemingway and Mark Twain. Take your pick. What this means is that you don't have to have lived in Uruguay to write about Uruguay. It means you need to visit Uruguay, do research on Uruguay, or interview some Uruguayans. Then, connecting with the internal emotional reservoir you've developed from being a person who lives somewhere, and armed with your new knowledge, you write.

This book is not a writing manual, nor is it a grammar book. It is a *writing group guide*. I will suggest books, conferences, and online sources that cover the basics of how to write. I will share tips we've learned along the way on writing, but I am not an expert. At the time of this writing, I have had five years of hands-on experience developing and refining a writing group. This I have lived, and I know. In *All Write*, I will show you how you can create a group where members have an investment in one another's writing, where members have a genuine respect for one another's work. I will show you how to get past the urge to be nice and not hurt anyone's feelings, to helping one another go deeper in the writing process in a kind and respectful way. While your group will not be a mirror image of my group, I will cover the basics of what a group needs in general to work well.

It takes a substantial commitment to create a positive group experience, one in which members don't merely add or take away commas but help one another develop characters and storylines. Where members challenge one another with a respectful and supportive approach. Where at the end of a writers' group, members go home exhausted from the mental work (your brain uses 20 percent of your energy). Where members leave with a sense of accomplishment, a feeling of success, and new tools to take their writing up a notch. Where members see a clearer path ahead, and, curiously, have a surge of new energy.

I have written this book because we at Shoreline have what I consider a practical, user-friendly format for developing a writing group. While you will need to modify our approach to meet your own needs, this is a good stepping-off point. We motivate one another to delve deeper. We brainstorm ideas for one another's characters and storylines. We constructively critique, and we edit one another's work down to the last comma. We have created a level of discipline in our group that helps us hone our skills as we move our stories both forward and deeper.

How many writers does it take to write one book?
Our Answer: Four

Let's hear from our members about how a group has benefited them.

How I've Benefited from Shoreline Writers:

CLAIRE: I don't think I'd be writing without a writing group. They give me the discipline of deadlines, the guts to omit or add, and the fresh look at the chapter I'm sick of. When they praise a description or a plot or a metaphor, I preserve it. When they recommend omitting a phrase or a cliché or a point that doesn't move the story forward, I make the changes. When they say, "I'd like to know more about . . ." I make the addition. When we disagree, we talk it out without tension. I also have to admit there is a certain thrill to reading my creation to others who genuinely want me to succeed as a writer.

Not surprisingly, my writing group's feedback, our group exercises, and our annual retreats improve my writing. I make errors. I am not consistent. I overuse a word. At times my writing isn't clear, usually because my thinking isn't clear. My friends have caught all this. I love it. I'm becoming a better writer.

But surprising to me is the reward I get from giving

---

feedback. The thinking I've done when critiquing another member's work has become writing lesson after writing lesson, from the clear mechanics of grammar to the hazy understanding of an author's unique voice, which, by the way, has emerged for each one of us in the group.

Addendum: Not very often, but occasionally, I get in a writing slump. I can't seem to write anything I'm pleased with. I've discovered that talking about writing problems like this with the Shoreline Writers can turn me in the other direction. Somehow, articulating the problem and having the group listen and offer ideas is the antidote for me. At a recent meeting, I confessed my slump to the group at the start. Within the first half hour, I was surprisingly reinvigorated, not from pep talks, but from the power of camaraderie, a power I did not foresee.

DIANNE: Belonging to a writing group provides structure and deadlines, a must for me. Joining an existing group meant learning how to fit into an established, unique culture. I had some catching up to do. This group is more experienced than my first writing group, and it keeps us operating at a comfortably advanced level. Although I was initially an outsider, I did feel supported. The group nurtures a creative force in me that compels me to write. The weekly editing and critiquing of my work give me valuable insights into how to improve my writing. For me, other benefits of a writing group include camaraderie and the opportunity to read, edit, and critique members' writing, an enriching experience.

MARY: Not to discourage you, but I haven't pushed the *go button* on my manuscript. My group has been the voice of reason. Without them, I would have made the regrettable mistake of submitting my work to an agent before it was spit-shined and ready for consideration.

The group offers a higher consciousness. Collectively, we are a massive amount of brain cells united in a compassionate effort, critiquing one another's writing and offering creative paths not considered.

I would be lost without my group. They are my friends, coaches, and cheerleaders. They push me to meet deadlines and challenge me to do my best writing.

Most importantly, I've become a happy tribe member and work toward the success of all. Everyone's writing is important. I critique, research, and edit, and get the immense satisfaction of contributing to a garden of creative endeavors, not just my own budding book.

DEBBIE: In the four years since we began meeting, I have completed the first draft of a YA mystery, started a second novel, written numerous essays, crafted a short story which I have submitted for inclusion in an anthology, and started this book about writing groups. I would not have done any of this without the support of the group. Every week, my motivation to get writing is my "Midnight on Monday" deadline to send in my work for group on Wednesday. Having deadlines keeps me on track. Left to my own devices, I can find too many other things to do.

I don't find writing easy. At least I don't find writing well easy. I can let words flow onto the page, but to have them make sense, be consistent, tell a story in a timely fashion, that's a different story. Knowing I have my writing group there to let me know when, where, and even why I've gone astray is invaluable. They also tell me when something works, which boosts my confidence to keep going. Writing well is hard work. Having a group of like-minded souls who share the same passion and drive as I do makes the effort I've expended even more rewarding.

Being in a group works for each of us in powerful ways. We all agree that having deadlines to complete our writing each week keeps us on track. We all agree that receiving feedback, invaluable suggestions, and powerful insights from one another has helped us improve our writing skills. This in turn fuels our creative instincts, which morphs into more and better words, sentences, paragraphs, pages, chapters, and ultimately books. And finally, we all agree that reading, editing, and critiquing one another's book is as rewarding as getting input on our own work. We've learned that both being edited and doing editing propels us on our own paths.

One reason our group works so well is because we spend time learning and practicing the craft. We do this at our annual retreats and at meetings throughout the year. We choose a topic that interests us (for example—metaphors), one of us researches the subject and presents it to the group, then we create a writing exercise around it. Some of these exercises we do once or twice, while some we repeat numerous times.

I have included these group exercises in *All Write* at the end of each chapter. A few of the exercises are designed to help you create your group, and others are exercises we utilized to hone our writing skills. While I did not write this book to teach you how to write, I am sharing with you what has helped Shoreline Writers along the way.

That's what I can do best—show you how we have learned together. And hope these exercises help you as much as they have helped us.

What Do I Want from a Writing Group?

✓ **Find the right writing group**
✓ **Prep: Yes**

Purpose: This exercise is designed to help you home in on the type of group you are interested in forming or joining. It will explore specifically what you hope to get from a group.

Prep: Individual instructions: This exercise can be done for your own personal exploration or in preparation for forming a writing group with other prospective group members.

1. Write down the top three to five reasons you'd like to be in a writing group. If you've been in a writing group before, what worked? What didn't work? Use this experience as a guideline.
   - Are you actively writing a book and seeking a group for support and critiquing?
   - Are you excited to try your hand at writing and want a group to help you explore the basics?
   - Are you feeling isolated by writing on your own?
   - Do you feel you'd benefit from having some writing buddies?
2. List your preferences in terms of group size and structure:
   - Do you want to join a small group or a large one?
     - A small group ensures you get personal time at each meeting to share your writing.
     - A large group exposes you to many voices and lets you off the hook for sharing your writing at each meeting.
   - Do you want a peer group, a group with a leader, or to be the leader of a group?
     - A peer group will enable you to create your own process.

- A facilitated group allows you to step into an already structured setting.
    - Being the leader allows you to have some control over how the group is structured.
- Do you want a critique group where your work is read and edited by other group members as well as editing the work of others?
- Do you want a group that incorporates learning and/or practicing the craft of writing at meetings?
- Other things to consider:
    - In-person or virtual group
    - Meeting times
    - Whether groups have assignments between meeting times
    - Whether group members have experience with writing or are novices
    - Whether group members are writing in the same genre as you, or the group has a mix of genres

3. After your list is complete, let it be your compass in reaching out and creating, or joining your own, unique circle of peers.
    - Contact libraries in your area to see if there are existing groups, or if they are agreeable to having a group meet there.
    - Contact bookstores near you to see if there are writing groups that meet there, or if they would be agreeable to hosting one.
    - One way to meet other writers is to take a writing course. This can be at a local college, either for credit or in their Adult Learning program; at a Community or Adult Education Program, or in a privately run class.

Group instructions for the meeting: When you find a group of interested writers, you can use this exercise as a jumping off place to discuss what is important in forming a group.

CHAPTER TWO
The Top Ten Reasons Our Group Works

We will need to find people who will provide a safe writing space for us,
where criticism comes late, and love and delight come early.
—L.L. Barkat

1. It's Small

Four women started Shoreline Writers, and it didn't take us long to decide we wanted to keep our membership to four. The reason was strictly practical. We wanted enough time every week for each of us to share our writing, and because we spend several hours a week editing one another's work. A small group allows each of us enough time to work on our own writing, get feedback on our work, and help the other group members dig deeper with theirs. A larger group would dilute the intensity of our time together.

2. It's Leaderless

Some writing groups have a leader and participants. At Shoreline Writers, we are the leaders as well as the participants. Our group evolved this way from the beginning. Because we are small, having enough time for each member to read and receive feedback is easy to manage. Larger groups may find a leader is more practical in terms of time management.

We make decisions about how the group operates through discussion and consensus. And we all try to be flexible. One example of our flexibility is that when one member (and then a second member) began wintering in Florida, the group was willing to have our winter meetings via Skype. We attended a free Skype training program at our local library, and, for the cold months when our two snowbirds fly south, we have long distance meetings. When in person became impossible, Zoom was added to our repertoire of computer skills, and we became a virtual group overnight.

When tasks arise, they get done. One woman volunteered to write up our schedules and retreat agendas. Another member pulled out her phone and became the timekeeper. A third participant offered to host our annual retreat at her house the first year and has done so ever since.

No one is in charge. We make group decisions as issues arise. Spontaneity and flexibility within a structure has worked well for us.

3. Everyone's Invested

We invest a lot of time in Shoreline Writers. To have a successful group, we need to commit not only to our own writing, but to the group. We found it works best to have a four-hour weekly meeting, which gives each member an hour to share her work. Having this amount of time has helped us cultivate an intimacy which allows us to know one another and one another's work at a deep level.

It's empowering and comforting to know we have three other individuals who are invested in the outcome of our writing. They want it to be as good as it can be. We bounce ideas off one another about what works, what doesn't work, and what other avenues we might explore.

The four of us are also a built-in team of researchers. Each of us has a different field of expertise, and by sharing our knowledge we raise one another's skill level and database. One group member who likes to research everything often comes in with new tidbits to consider. Another member can explain why "-ing" words are not the best to use, where the commas should go, or when to use a semicolon. She is also our metaphor queen. One member shares her editing expertise, having taken additional editing courses. Another member has the most beautiful vocabulary and can string words together the rest of us would never consider. On the flip side, she runs our "chop shop," helping us trim away the needless words we tend to use.

We bring in resources and readings and ideas from conferences we've attended, books we've read, and online sources. Together we can cover more territory than any one of us could do individually. During the week, if we read something of interest, we email it to the group. This could be as simple as a Grammar Girl tip, or an article that addresses something in one of our writings, such as what ingredients were in Coca-Cola during the Gilded Age when the recipe for Coke was starkly different.

This peer support, as is true in any activity, keeps us motivated and moving forward in our writing. We don't let our fellow writers take it easy in telling their story. We push them to go as deeply as they can in the telling.

4. The Write Stuff

To have a writing group with this level of commitment means you must vet participants before they join. Initially, anyone who was interested in the group was included. Three of the four of us shared the same values—cooperation, not competition. The member who did not left of her own accord within a short while.

The three of us continued for about a year before we decided to consider including another member. While we were working well together, three people is too small a number for a group. If one person can't make it, the group can't happen. We discussed the traits and qualities that we thought were important for a new member. We based our list on what our group was focused on at the time. Every group will be different. You will have a different list. The important piece is that you know the type of group you want, which will guide you in how to include members.

We wanted someone who shared our goal of writing a book and was
- Knowledgeable in the craft of writing, not a beginner;
- A good listener;
- Open-minded;
- Interested in doing the level of editing and writing we were doing, with the time to do it;
- Willing to be vulnerable and daring;
- Good at giving and taking constructive feedback;
- Passionate about writing;
- Well-read;
- Cooperative and supportive in helping all group members achieve their goal.

We agreed that a current member would have to vouch for a new member and that there would be a trial period to see if everyone worked well together. When we approached our prospective fourth member, we presented her with how we operated to ensure she was willing to do the work. But remember: Whether you're starting a group from scratch or adding a new member, it takes time for the trust and cohesion to grow. It also takes a willingness to be open and vulnerable as well as having a deep commitment to the process. Finally, and we can't stress this enough, it takes a lot of work on everyone's part.

5. We're Cohesive

Early on in our group, we realized our weekly meeting was not conducive to getting to know one another on a personal level. Because we were focused on our writing and editing, which was all good, we didn't have the time to get to know the first thing about one another's lives. We decided to have a retreat to build cohesiveness which is important to group dynamics. It is now a yearly event. Hosted by one of our members, we spend a full day (ten to four thirty) doing a variety of writing exercises, exploring some aspect of our craft, sharing our writing, and, of utmost importance, walking to a local restaurant for lunch. It has proven to be both a day of learning and a day of bonding.

We occasionally attend writing seminars and conferences together to hone our writing skills. We've taken field trips to scope out the setting of a member's book. When one grandmother in the group had unexpected babysitting duties, we moved our meeting from the library to her home. If someone has a conflict on our meeting day, we do our best to reschedule so everyone can be there. It doesn't always work, but we always try.

6. Goals

Our Group Goal is simple: To actively support one another's writing goals.

This is not as elementary as it sounds. Each member needs to be both a dedicated giver and open receiver of feedback. We don't achieve our group goal if a member doesn't actively give ideas to other members, or if a member doesn't welcome ideas on her own work.

Good goals are supposed to have measures of success and a timetable for achieving them. Well, we don't have either. Our group goal isn't measurable; it's subjective. Our only measure of success is the level of satisfaction of each member.

Our individual goals are more challenging. At our retreats, we each create a personal goal for the year. Out of our individual goals, we come up with an individual mantra, which we use to help us stay focused. Our mantras and goals reflect what we need to concentrate on in the coming year in terms of our writing, our book, or ourselves as writers.

Here is a sample of members' individual goals and mantras.

DIANNE: Goal: Submit *Rule of Five* to an agent by the end of the year.
Mantra: Fini

CLAIRE: Goal: Carve ten nonnegotiable hours out each week for writing book and sculpt *Georgiana* out of facts found.
Mantra: Carve

MARY: Goal: Before our next retreat in June 2019, complete *Cockeyed* and bring manuscript for each member to edit.
Mantra: Unexpected Destiny

DEBBIE: Goal: Make *All Write* happen.
Mantra: All Write!

7. Discipline Drives the Day

One of the members of our group is a retired banker, and she often says, "Deadlines drive the process." Deadlines create a discipline, which is important in establishing a group work ethic. And yes, it is work. We have a responsibility to one another to edit and critique one another's work every week. But there is never any pressure to produce. We all have scheduling issues that may interfere with our ability to find time to write, or we're doing research that particular week, or we just have to take a break. But we have a commitment to make the time to read and edit the other members' work. We come prepared. To be less than prepared is to let down our sister writers (our group is all women only because that's who signed up). We have expectations of one another which we take seriously.

8. Conscientious Critiquing

Becoming a good editor is a process. In Chapter Three we discuss how to approach editing, which is important, but maybe even more so is how to deliver our critique. Early on, we did not want to hurt anyone's feelings, so we tiptoed around with our feedback. Commenting on commas and grammar was easy. Telling someone you didn't like or understand a passage was not.

Learning how to frame a constructive comment about content was a challenging experience. It took a while to develop our sea legs. How you give feedback can be dangerous, like hidden rocks just under the surface of the water.

Okay, maybe that's a bit too strong, but imagine you've just poured your heart into ten pages of the most brilliant, inspired writing. Then *poof!* someone says, "You know, that really doesn't make any sense to me." Trust me, we say that now. But initially we were trepidatious about hurting feelings, probably because we were worried our feelings were about to be hurt. It took us a while to realize, *No one's telling me I'm not a good writer; no one's telling me I'm wrong; no one's criticizing me. They're helping me figure it out. What a gift! They're being honest and working with me, not against me!*

Members' different perspectives add to the richness of the group experience, which enhances everyone's writing. To sum up, receiving and giving constructive criticism is:

- About writing and sharing that writing
- About getting feedback on how your words impact the others in your group
- About being vulnerable
- About getting lots of praise
- And lots of encouragement
- And lots of help
- And best of all, **it works**!

9. We Leave Our Judgments at the Door

We have respect for one another's writing style, content, and characters. And we agree there is no right or wrong, no good or bad. No judgments are allowed in our editing, our critiquing, or our meetings. We can agree with the author's style, content, and voice, or we can disagree with it. We can voice our opinions about what we think will make it better, stronger, deeper, but it is *only our opinion,* and this is crucial to the success of the group. We try to be well-informed about why something works for us, or doesn't work, but we're clear it is just our perspective.

We also are careful in how we word our feedback. Here are some of our favorite openers:

- What would you think about . . . ?
- Would you consider . . . ?
- I like that, but what about . . . ?
- Would it work to . . . ?
- I may not be right, but what about . . . ?

Respect is a crucial element for any group. It's no different than what makes a business partnership or a personal relationship work. Not imposing one's beliefs on another, accepting the other person exactly where they are, and holding genuine respect for them are of paramount importance to the effectiveness of any relationship. Which leads us right into reason number ten.

10. R-E-S-P-E-C-T

Being open to hearing one another's comments, suggestions, and critiques of our work opens new pathways, new possibilities for us to consider in our writing. It's a delicate process. Sometimes it's an immediate *Aha, why didn't I see that?* Other times we're so in love with what we've written, the thought of changing a word of it seems beyond our ability to comprehend. Other times, once we're at home going over the work, we think, *Oh, yeah, that really would work better.*

But ultimately the decision of what is to be written, what is to be kept, what is to be cut or changed is the choice of the writer. We respect this process. We have free rein to say our piece, but never lose sight of the fact that the author has the final say as to what words will go on the page. Which is exactly as it should be.

Guidelines to Come Together

✓ **Build a cohesive writing group**
✓ **Prep: Yes**

Purpose: This exercise is designed to help you focus on what is important both to the individual members and the group as a whole in creating a successful alliance.

Prep: Individual instructions prior to the group meeting:
1. Make a list of five things you *want* from and five things you can *offer* to your writing group (see Exercise 1). Your answers may be the same or different. This list should include anything and everything that you think is important.
2. Bring your list to the meeting.

Materials for group: Each member brings their individual lists. One member brings poster board and markers.

Group instructions for the meeting:
1. Choose a person to chart the *wants* and *offerings* responses in two separate columns.
2. Each member reads their two lists aloud.
3. Put checks next to ideas that are repeated.
4. Discuss.
5. Prioritize the top five in each group based on the number of checks the item receives.
6. Determine if the group is open to using these ten ideas as the temporary guidelines for the group.
7. Reassess in six months, one year, or at your retreats.

CHAPTER THREE
Immerse Yourself in a Group Retreat

Alone we can do so little, together we can do so much.
—Helen Keller

Since we formed Shoreline Writers, we have held a retreat each spring. It's an effective way to get to know one another more intimately. While we focus our day around writing and writing exercises, the informality of being at a member's home (weather permitting, on her backyard deck) allows for a sharing of more than just our written words. Our lunchtime stroll to a local eatery gives us the opportunity to talk about other aspects of our lives we don't usually have time for.

The first time we held a retreat, we did not know much about one another, so we intentionally incorporated team-building exercises. The first exercise from that first retreat involved each member writing one sentence of a story and passing it on to the next person until it went around the group three times. This "Pass-Around-Story" exercise has become our standard retreat opener. The twists and turns always make us laugh. Each year we rotate who sets the scene with the opening sentence, and who must pen the grand finale. While we're writing the story, we don't discuss what direction we're taking it. With three people writing ahead of you, it goes off into unimaginable tangents before it returns to you. Instructions can be found in Group Exercise 4 at the end of this chapter.

Here is our Pass-Around-Story from last year.

Retreat Pass-Around-Story 2018

Mary: My name really isn't Isabella.

Debbie: That was my grandmother's name and before she died, she asked me to use it.

Claire: But my mother would have never named me that—and she didn't.

Dianne: The name has changed me, changed everything.

Mary: It's made me question my marriage, my job, and myself.

Debbie: It's as if Grandma Isabella comes to me in my dreams and reprograms the circuitry of my very being.

Claire: But now I wish I'd never taken it.

Dianne: There is only one way to manipulate this mess that will keep me out of prison.

Mary: I've got no choice but to confess to my grandmother's crimes. The money she stole. The jewelry she hid.

Debbie: Maybe if I do, her soul will finally be at rest, and she'll leave me alone to live my own life.

Claire: But where can I hide the money and jewelry that I've stolen over the years?

Dianne: Her urn!

Besides this exercise, we have several other team-building exercises which can be found at the end of this chapter.

Prior to retreat day, we decide which writing topic(s) we would like to focus on. One member offers to lead a discussion about a topic. Writing topics that we've focused on include: "Show, Don't Tell," Hemingway's "Tip of the Iceberg" writing theory, applying psychic distance in writing, and how to create a writing toolkit.

Here is a sample agenda:

Shoreline Writers Retreat—June 13, 2018, 10:00–4:30
Mary's House
Dianne, Deb, Mary, Claire

Prior to the retreat:
1. Read Hemingway's "Big Two-Hearted River." This will be used in a writing exercise. [Group Exercise 13, Chapter Nine.]
2. Select and print a photograph of a scene of your choice. Write a one-page short story using the photo as the setting for a character's reaction to a situation they are in. Write the story from the perspective of a dangerous person, a nervous person, a monk, or your protagonist. [Group Exercise 9, Chapter Five.]

Materials to bring to the retreat:
1. Copy of Hemingway's story
2. Your photograph and four copies of your short story
3. Pad to write on
4. Pencils/pens
5. Snacks/drinks
6. This agenda

Agenda:
- **Pass-Around-Story** [Group Exercise 4, Chapter Three]
  - Led by Debbie (thirty minutes)
  - To start the exercise, one person writes the opening line.
  - Pass the paper to the left.
  - That person writes the next sentence and passes it left.
  - Go around the group three times or until an established time period is up.
  - The person who writes the last line reads the story aloud.
- **Tip-of-the-Iceberg exercise** [Group Exercise 13, Chapter Nine]
  - Led by Debbie (one hour)
- **Active vs. Passive;** using "-ing" verbs vs. other tenses
  - Led by Grammar Claire (thirty minutes)

- **Lunch**
  - (ninety minutes)
- **Show-it Short Story exercise**: [Group Exercise 9, Chapter Seven]
  - Led by Dianne (sixty minutes)
- **Shoreline Writers' Writing Guide**
  - Led by Mary (sixty minutes)
    - » Review last retreat's poster on ingredients for good writing and update.
    - » Brainstorm our book idea: How to run a writing group.
    - » Brainstorm Salon idea: Salons for people wanting to start writing groups.
- **2018 Goals and Plans**
  - Led by Claire (thirty minutes)
  - Goals: Group and individual
  - Mantras
  - Schedule for 2019
  - Ideas for road trips

Let's hear from our members about their first retreat experience.

DEBBIE: What I remember most about our first retreat is how important it was to get to know the others as people, not just group members. And each year the retreat brings our connection deeper, just like our stories!

CLAIRE: I remember feeling a new lightness of friendship that made me comfortable from then on with getting and giving feedback. Weekly meetings can be intense, and this retreat broke that pattern.

MARY: Our retreat is like the Fourth of July. We come together to celebrate our friendship, strengthen our bonds, and share in the excitement of learning new writing techniques.

DIANNE: The annual retreat nurtures growth. A lively vibe of anticipation sets the mood—we are eager. An ambitious agenda sets the schedule—we are focused. A format of group participation fosters collaboration—we bond. We work and we learn and we grow.

Plan Your Retreat

✓ **Planning a retreat**
✓ **Prep: No**

Purpose: This exercise is designed to help your group plan a retreat that will foster team building and writing skills.

Group instructions for the meeting: Use the following suggested format and create a retreat agenda that meets your group's needs.

1. Choose one person to record the agenda and email the schedule to group members.
2. Decide on the following:
   * date
   * time
   * location
   * what to bring:
     ○ computers or no computers
     ○ paper and pens
3. Set an agenda:
   * icebreaker and warm-up exercises to start the retreat
     ○ select exercises
     ○ facilitator
     ○ time allotted
   * writing topics to be presented
     ○ select topics
     ○ facilitator
     ○ time allotted
   * group exercises
     ○ select exercises
     ○ facilitator

- o time allotted
- discuss Group Exercise 2 (Ten Tactics to Come Together)
  - o facilitator
  - o how is the group working?
  - o what things need to be changed?
    - » ideas for what the change(s) should look like and how it/they should be implemented
- goals and mantras
  - o facilitator
  - o set a group goal at the retreat for the coming year
  - o share individual goals and mantras for the coming year
    - » members should prepare a personal goal and mantra prior to the meeting
- set a schedule for the coming year
  - o meeting days and times
- discuss ideas for road trips related to subjects you are researching or writing conferences to attend

Pass-Around-Story

✓ **Collaborative story writing**
✓ **Prep: No**

Purpose: This exercise is designed as an icebreaker for a new group, or a warm-up exercise for your retreat. It allows members to get a glimpse of the inner workings of one another's writing styles and personalities, while being a simple and fun exercise.

Group instructions for the meeting: The group writes one collaborative story by taking turns writing individual sentences until the story is complete.

1. Establish the number of turns (three – five) for each member.
2. One member writes the opening line.
   - be creative
   - incomplete sentences are fine
   - have fun with it
3. The story is passed to the left and that member writes the next sentence. This continues until each member has had the established number of turns.
4. The last person writes the last line.
5. Read the story out loud when you're finished.
6. Save it! It's fun to reread each year to see how the group has evolved.

Group critique: No critiquing allowed here. This is purely for fun!

Descriptive Writing

✓ **Descriptive writing**
✓ **Prep: No**

Purpose: This exercise is designed to help you develop the skill of descriptive writing. Descriptions are important in storytelling; how you write them can make or break a story.

Materials for group: Each member brings a small object from home concealed in a paper bag.

Group instructions for the meeting: Write a descriptive narrative about one another's objects. Pass your object in its bag to the group member on your left.

1. Open the bag you receive and look at the object without the other members seeing it.
2. Sit silently and ponder the object for one minute.
3. Describe the object in writing without identifying what it is. Write for three minutes. Make your description vivid and visceral. Include your thoughts, feelings, and sensory perceptions about this item. Or write about what it evokes in you, your personal experience with the object. Use imagery. The rules are loose for this exercise. Just write.
4. Pass the item in its bag to the person on your left.
5. Repeat steps #2 through #5 until each member has had an opportunity to write about every object. Stop when the object reaches its owner. The owner of the object does not write about it.
6. Discuss each object:
    - The owner of the object to be discussed places it on the table.

- Each member reads their narrative aloud.
- Compare and contrast the descriptions written by the various group members.

Group critique: The group provides feedback as to what worked and discusses other techniques the author might include in terms of helping the reader get the full experience of the writer's intention.

Create a Writer's Toolkit

✓ **Develop a toolkit of writing resources**
✓ **Prep: Yes**

Purpose: This exercise is designed to help you improve writing skills by brainstorming tried and true resources used by group members.

Prep: Individual instructions prior to the group meeting: Compose a list of resources you have found helpful in your writing process. These resources can include dictionaries, writing style guides, books on writing, websites, blogs, conferences attended, writers you follow on social media, trainings, exercises you've found helpful, and anything else related to writing.

Materials for group: Each member brings their list of resources. One member brings poster board and markers.

Group instructions for the meeting: As a group, list the tools and the resources that will help you hone your writing skills.

1. Choose one member to record the resources.
2. Group members share the resources they have found useful in writing.
3. Decide which dictionary to use if your group is critiquing one another's works. In the editing world, *Merriam-Webster's Collegiate Dictionary* is often the dictionary of choice.
4. Choose a writing style guide for the group to use. The most commonly used style guides are the *Chicago Manual of Style* for writing fiction and nonfiction; the *Associated Press AP Stylebook* for journalism; the *Modern Language Association's MLA Handbook* for journals and academia; and *The Elements of Style* for a basic but thorough guide to clear, concise, and proper writing.
5. After the meeting, one member organizes the list and makes copies for all members.

PART TWO

A Group Helps the Writer Evolve

For some authors, writing seems to flow effortlessly onto the page. Some say their words emanate from their higher self, while others say their books are driven by the characters. Jack Kerouac said that great writers, such as Whitman, Melville, and Thoreau, are geniuses born with the gift to write. For some the first draft hardly needs revision; all the elements of plot, character development, and story arc are there. Take Ulysses S. Grant, for example. Penniless and dying of throat cancer, he agreed to write a memoir so his wife would not be left destitute. Ron Chernow in *Grant* (New York: Penguin Press, 2017, pp. xviii-xix) writes: "As seen in his wartime orders, [Grant] had had patented a lean, supple writing style, and a crisp narrative now flowed in polished sentences, honed by the habits of a lifetime." While in excruciating pain, Grant wrote an amazing "336,000 words of superb prose in a year" (ibid.). Toward the end of his life, when he could no longer write, he "dictated at one sitting a nine-thousand-word portrait of Lee's surrender at Appomattox 'never pausing, never hesitating for a word, never repeating—and [according to Mark Twain, his publisher] in the written-out copy he made hardly a correction'" (ibid., pp. xix-xx).

None of the Shoreline Writers were born with the genius or the gift. We all felt we had a book inside of us, but we didn't know how to get it onto the page in a shape that could be published. When we first met at the university memoir writing course, Mary had the first draft of a novel completed and was attending the class to find out how to get it published. I had coauthored a nonfiction book and was looking to start writing fiction. Claire had been saying for years that she was going to write about her great-grandmother but had yet to begin. Dianne had been toying with ideas about writing but needed the discipline to sit down and do it.

Each of us had come to this point of feeling the pull to write a book from different directions. Happily, our paths converged, and we discovered: a) it's a lot of hard work, b) we had a lot to learn, and c) we could figure it out together.

The members of our group are determined to be the best writers we can be. As amateurs, we quickly realized we had to get back to basics. (Remember your English teacher drawing sentence diagrams on the board?) To that end, we now dedicate time to writing exercises to hone our skills. This, we believe, is a large part of what makes our group hit the mark.

In the next several chapters I will discuss techniques we used in our group to help us write more evocatively and expressively. I'll give an overview of these various concepts and share the exercises we have created and utilized to refine our abilities. These writing assignments are intended as a jumping off point for you and your group. Soon you'll be editing ours, adapting them for your particular needs, and creating your own!

CHAPTER FOUR

Carving Out Time to Write

I can shake off everything as I write;
my sorrows disappear, my courage is reborn.
—Anne Frank

Chiseling out a chunk of time in your day to sit down and write can feel daunting. However, if you don't pencil time in your schedule, you most likely won't get a book written. To get that book out of your head and onto the page means you must make writing a priority. Yet you also must be flexible enough to accommodate your life as a householder, a worker, a parent, a spouse, a partner, a grandparent, or any other role.

So, what are you going to stop doing? You have to make choices about how you spend your time. But, the joy of writing, as Anne Frank so beautifully expressed, hooks you. It's a feel-good experience, and one you'll enjoy so much, you won't mind giving up some of your other activities.

Let's hear from our members on how they carved out time for writing.

DEBBIE: Having just retired, I was able to easily slip into the deliciousness of sitting and writing. But to keep the time free, I had to turn down many other opportunities such as volunteer work, book clubs, and hardest of all, lunches out with friends.

CLAIRE: I was in five monthly book clubs and I dropped three of them, substituting one passion for another. I wish I could do it all, but I had to choose.

MARY: I put down my paintbrush in order to find time to write the book my dying mother told me I should write.

When your mother tells you to do something, you listen. Writing a novel was never on my bucket list. I've always been one to fling paint on a canvas to tell a story. The experience of telling a story using words is all consuming and much harder than I could have known—yet, in some ways, more satisfying.

DIANNE: When I joined the group, I was not working outside the home. But that didn't make it easy to carve out time. With three teenage children and a home to run, finding enough hours to write was challenging. I had to organize my responsibilities and then give myself permission to take time for myself. A hard thing for a mother to do.

One of the many gifts from working together is that the group is a major support, helping each of us manage this balancing act. We can bounce ideas off one another. Or if one of us is overwhelmed in her life, she can take a break without anyone at Shoreline begrudging her that time off. There are not many places in life where we can do this so effortlessly.

Carving Out Time to Write

✓ **Schedule time for your writing**
✓ **Prep: Yes**

Purpose: This exercise is designed to assist group members in planning out a personal schedule which includes time to write, edit, and attend group meetings.

Prep: Individual instructions prior to the group meeting: Look at your weekly work, householder, and personal schedules, then chisel out chunks of time to write, to edit one another's writing, and to attend group meetings.

1. Plan out your writing schedule.
2. Be realistic about how many hours you can devote to writing.
3. Look at what other commitments you have that are inviolate.
4. Consider activities that take up your time that you can let go of.
5. Write down your schedule to bring to your meeting.
   - Example:
     - ○ Monday is a *Writing Day*: two to three hours.
     - ○ Tuesday is an *Editing Day*: other's work-in-progress (WIP), four hours.
     - ○ Wednesday is a *Group Day*: four hours.
     - ○ Thursday is a *Post-Group Editing Day*: my WIP, one to two hours.
     - ○ Friday is a *day off*.
     - ○ Saturday is a *Writing Day*: two to three hours.
     - ○ Sunday is a *Writing Day*: two to three hours.

Materials for group: Each member brings their writing schedule.

Group instructions for the meeting: Members share their schedules with the group and discuss any challenges they face in setting aside time. Brainstorm ideas to help create time. Share ideas that have worked for each of you. This is where you get creative and create a plan that works for all of you.

CHAPTER FIVE
Sitting Down to Write

It's not about making the right choice.
It's about making a choice and making it right.
—J.R. Rim

Decisions, decisions, decisions

There are decisions you need to make about your story before you begin writing. These determinations are essential. That's not to say we made them all; but we learned their value along the way! I'm sure you've heard what builders have to say about renovating an old house—it's easier to do a teardown and build a new one. Renovating a completed book and shoring up the foundation after you've built the three-story house atop it is painful. But if you follow your blueprint and include structural essentials such as **genre**, **audience**, **time frame**, **setting**, **point of view**, and **tense**, your creation will be solid and viable.

Genre/Audience

Before you sit down to write, here are several important **decisions** for you to make. What **genre** of book do you want to write? What do you like to read? Is historical fiction your milieu? Mystery? Thriller? Romance? Nonfiction? Sci-fi? Memoir? Reading a lot in whatever genre you are interested in is helpful for knowing what is expected from that type of read. If you're writing romance, there has to be a happy ending. If you're writing a mystery, there has to be a dead body. If you're writing a thriller, you have to get your readers on the edge of their seats. Readers of specific genres expect certain things from the books they read, and you better deliver! So be clear on what type of book you want to write.

Next, who is your **audience?** Do you want to write for young adults? Adults? Children? Once you decide these two important criteria, genre and general audience, then it's time to explore who your target audience is, and what types of books are in demand. Even if you have a close-to-complete idea in your head, further clarifying these two points will prove helpful.

Understanding the market will help you focus your book in a certain direction. If you're writing purely for your own pleasure, however, this is not important. In our circle, Claire is writing for her family members and self-publishes. For her, knowing the market is not important. However, for the three of us who want to find a publisher, we had to do some work in this area. Mary is writing fiction for the adult female population and wants to be published. Dianne is writing a how-to book for pregnant or want-to-be pregnant women about how to promote brain strength in babies. She also is interested in being published. I started with a young adult mystery, then moved to adult fiction, and then to this nonfiction book, *All Write*, which I have self-published. I hope to return to the YA mystery and publish that as well. It helps to know your niche, to know where to focus your effort when trying to get an agent, the first step in getting published.

Research your topic

Once you're clear on the genre of your book and your audience, consider the **time frame** of the story and the **location**. These are key elements of establishing the **setting**, the world your characters inhabit. This means it is time to start your **research**, which will be an ongoing process for the duration of your writing. Whether you're writing fiction or nonfiction, you need to be well versed in your subject matter.

At a writing conference which I attended, one presenter said that every first book is autobiographical in some way. We at Shoreline Writers can attest to the truth in that statement (adolescent trauma for me, pregnancy for Dianne, family lineage for Claire, and a mother's dying wish for Mary). If this is your first book, you'll likely think you know your subject very well as it's in some way based on you, but there will still be areas you need to explore in more depth. For the two of us writing fiction, we were surprised by how much research we had to do; we investigated topics as diverse as powerboats, amblyopia (lazy-eye), Texas, Vietnam, and hospitals in the Wild West. Claire, who writes about her ancestors, is spending hours upon hours upon hours doing research, as is Dianne, who is devouring everything she can on the impact of a mother's choices in areas such as eating and exercising on having a smart child. The goal of this research is not to put it all in the book, but to

steep yourself in the information so it is reflected in your words. You will use all this information to set the scene for the reader. As an added benefit, research gives you new ideas and a new vocabulary.

Immerse yourself in your topic. Google it. Read books about it. Watch movies from the time period. Travel to places you are writing about, if possible. These are good ways to **absorb** the geography, politics, local atmosphere, history, and culture of an area. Talk with and listen to people who experienced an event or live in an area you are writing about. They have much to offer. Your local historical society and library have volumes of information about the time period you're writing about that are not available online. And don't forget museums.

> *TIP from Claire: Before approaching anyone by phone or in person, prepare a list of questions in writing. Do this for yourself. That way you will have a crisp, thorough, well-articulated question that doesn't overwhelm the person you're asking.*

Remember to fact check your work as you go. It's embarrassing to write a passage about your protagonist watching a cardinal sitting in a snow-covered pine tree in 1940s Boston, have the book published, and then find out that cardinals had not made it as far north as Massachusetts yet. True story! James Benn, a published author who is coincidently married to Debbie, now even researches the flora and fauna he includes in his books.

Let's hear from our members on how they do research.

> **DEBBIE:** One of my favorite research outings I took was for my young adult novel. I went to a local museum which had a retrospective of the John Meyer clothing line from the fifties and sixties. He was local to the area where I grew up, and everyone went to his back-to-school sales! It was so much fun

to see my favorite outfits from junior high and high school. The goal of my trip: to properly dress my teenage protagonist.

MARY: I do two distinctive kinds of research, one for knowledge and the other for style.

Knowledge-based research gives me the ammo to be an armchair expert, so what I write about is credible. This kind of research helps me make decisions about the direction my story may, or may not take, and the actions and dialogue of my characters. It's the glue that holds my story together.

Style-based research, on the other hand, greases the wheels. It transports me out of my own sphere to consider other options. I use information gleaned from websites like a thesaurus to find juicy words to use, or www.writersdigest.com for advice to pump up style and character development.

CLAIRE: I probably explicitly use 5 percent of the facts I gather—just the tip of the iceberg. The other 95 percent is all below the surface. (We'll be talking about Hemingway's Iceberg Theory in a later chapter.)

DIANNE: Research is a black hole that'll compress long hours of work into mere minutes of useful information where numerous pages of data amount to one teensy sentence with one weensy citation. It's a bit maddening. I need to remind myself of its importance, so I don't get discouraged.

Point of View

Early in the process, you need to decide which **point of view** (POV) to write from. Point of view is the perspective from which the story is told. We grappled with this concept a lot, especially during the first few years. We had many, many group discussions about POV and how to maintain a consistent one. With practice it's become easier to do, but it is still something we monitor amongst ourselves. Here is our "Reader's Digest Condensed" version of what helped us understand it.

There are three types of POV:

- **First Person POV** has the protagonist telling the story. You write using the first-person pronoun "I" and "my." This is a powerful voice in that it draws the reader in, but it's challenging in that you can only write about what your character witnesses, hears, or knows. The protagonist cannot get inside another character's head. Everything that happens in the story happens through this person's perspective.
- **Second Person POV** is generally only used in instructional materials. You write from this POV using the second person pronoun "you."
- **Third Person POV** is broken down into three types: Limited, Multiple, and Omniscient. In this approach, the narrator is not one of the characters, but is an onlooker telling the story from one or more of the character's perspectives. All three third-person POVs use the third-person pronouns "he," "she," and "they."
  - **Third Person Limited** is told from the perspective of only one character. This is restrictive in that they must know what is going on to tell it in the story.
  - **Third Person Multiple** is told from the perspective of several characters, expanding what you can show happening in the story. If you choose this modality, you must be careful to let the reader know when the voice is coming from a different character. This is primarily done with a scene break or a new chapter.
  - **Third Person Omniscient** allows the narrator to know everything that is going on, even when other characters don't know it. It's like when you were a kid and you were sure your mother knew everything you did.

We each write from a different POV. Claire, writing about her ancestors, writes primarily from third person omniscient. She can tell the story from all different perspectives. She also utilizes the first person POV when she inserts her thoughts and opinions into her story. Mary, in her novel, writes from third person multiple; she vacillates between half a dozen different characters telling the story, usually separating them by chapters, but also using scene changes within a chapter. My young adult novel uses the first person POV, and my adult novel is third person multiple POV, alternating between two main characters. Dianne uses second person POV in her how-to book on pregnancy. Many writers combine different points of view in one book, which is also okay. If you choose this route, the important thing is that you make it clear to your reader who is making the observation, pondering, speaking. This is best accomplished by having the POV change in a chapter, or in a new scene. In general, once you establish a POV or multiple POVs, be consistent.

Tense

The next step is figuring out what **tense** you want to set your story in—past or present.

- **Present Tense**: Most young adult books are written in the present tense to create a sense of immediacy that will pull the readers in. Other fiction can also be written in the present tense.
- **Past Tense**: Most adult fiction is written in the past tense. But you can choose whichever tense you want; again, just be sure to be consistent throughout the book.

Sitting Down to Write

✓ **Preparing to write**
✓ **Prep: Yes**

Purpose: This exercise is designed to help you get started writing. You will explore various factors that need to be considered before you put pen to paper or fingers to keyboard. Don't worry. Your choices can always be changed.

Prep: Individual instructions prior to the group meeting: Consider genre, audience, point of view, tense, setting, and protagonist as they pertain to your book or short story. While you may know the answers to many of these questions, the answers tend to evolve over time, so this exercise is useful regardless of whether you have begun writing or are in the planning stage.

1. Consider the following questions:
   - What genre does the book or short story you want to write fall under?
     - biography
     - crime fiction
     - dystopia
     - fan fiction
     - fantasy
     - fiction
     - historical fiction
     - horror
     - literary fiction
     - memoir
     - mystery
     - narrative nonfiction

- romance
- science fiction
- self-help
- spiritual
- thriller
- western
- Who is your target audience?
  - Adult
    - » identify the specific adult group you have in mind (e.g. male, female, binary, new mothers, retired military, etc.)
  - new adult (ages 18-24 or 18-30)
  - young adult (ages 12-18)
  - middle grade (ages 9-12)
  - children (under age 9)
- What time period(s) is your book set in?
- Where does your story take place?
- What point(s) of view (POV) do you want to write from? Some authors combine different POVs, but you must be consistent in how it is done.
  - first person (I, me, my)
  - second person (you - usually reserved for writing manuals)
  - third person, which has three subsections (he, she, they)
    - » third person limited (from one character's perspective)
    - » third person multiple (from several characters' perspectives)
    - » third person omniscient (from all characters' perspectives)
- What tense do you want to write in?
  - past
  - present
  - past and present
- How do you imagine your protagonist, or if nonfiction, the character you are depicting?

- physical appearance
- voice: include accent, tone, verbosity or reticence, volume
- backstory
- personality
- quirks and idiosyncrasies
- motivations
- desires
- Write a paragraph or two about *who, what, where, when, why,* and the *how* of the story. This will give you and your group a brief overview of where you are heading. You don't have to know the whole story to write this. Just jot down some general parameters.

Materials for group: Each member brings a copy of their responses to the group meeting.

Group instructions for the meeting:
1. Members share their overviews.
2. After each person shares, the group can help you brainstorm and fill in the gaps in your story.

CHAPTER SIX
Useful Tips for You, the Writer

The art of writing is the art of applying
the seat of the pants to the seat of the chair.
—Mary Heaton Vorse

What type of writer are you?

How are you going to approach writing your book? Are you a **pantser** or an **outliner**? A pantser is someone who writes by the seat of their pants; they sit down at the computer and let the story flow onto the page. An outliner is going to outline the book first and make sure everything is in order before they put the first words on the page. There's no right or wrong here. Everyone has their own preferences. You may try writing what comes into your head and, after nothing makes sense, swear you're going to outline the next time. Or you may try outlining this time, but never look at the outline once you've written it. You will figure it out. Experiment with different approaches. See what works for you. In our group, we have both pantsers and outliners.

Voice
AUTHOR VOICE

You, the writer, bring your own **voice** to your story. Some of the ways an author conveys their voice are through sentence construction, tone, pace, plot devices, seriousness versus humor, amount of dialogue, and wordiness. Think of your favorite authors and how you've come to identify them by their style, regardless of which book of theirs you're reading. That is their voice. It is unique to them, the author. For example, if you're a mystery fan, you'd never confuse Robert Parker's sparse and pithy voice with Agatha Christie's dense and descriptive one.

Over the course of our time together at Shoreline Writers, we have all discovered our voices. None of us planned what we would sound like; rather, our writing is a reflection of at least one aspect of who we are, or even who we'd like to be. Stephen King has told us how scared he was of his own shadow as a youngster. And look at his voice! We've also become attuned to one another's voices, so that when we edit, we can do it in their particular voice, not our own.

CHARACTER VOICE

Voice is imparted to the character(s) by you, the author. You alone decide how you want your main characters to present themselves, although many authors claim the characters create themselves on the page. Even when that is the case, you will (at least in part) establish their voice through language, vocabulary, and tone; as well as by their age, vocation, avocation, social status, cultural background, how they dress, geographical location, quirkiness, seriousness, whether they are introverted or extroverted, compassionate or callous, and even through their silence. For us, this is a fun part of writing—figuring out who each character is and imbuing them with distinct qualities and idiosyncrasies. Consistency, however, is mandatory!

Tips for Writing

Now it's time to start writing. You've completed all the necessary steps. You know **who** the main cast of characters is. You know **what** you want to write about. You know **where** the story is set. You know **when** the story takes place. You have a general idea, if you're a pantser, **why** and **how** your character will do the things she does. If you're an outliner, you have a plan about her motivations and actions. Finally, you get to sit down at the computer. You've been thinking about this book for a long time. Now what?

- **A strong opening sentence, paragraph, chapter.** You've probably heard that the first line has to be powerful enough to hook the reader. You've heard the same advice about the first paragraph and the first chapter. And while it's true that those first sentences and paragraphs and pages are important, our tip: Don't get too hung up on them. Because you know what? What we've learned is that when you've finished your book, you will likely need to go back and rewrite that chapter. Our advice: Sit down and write! Edits and rewrites are a constant, and that's okay, but the important thing is to keep moving forward, a word, a paragraph, a page, a chapter at a time.

- **Chart the details in your story** as you're writing. Keep track of your timeline, scenes and other pertinent information. Do any of your characters speak with a particular dialect? Keep track of the words they use, the spelling, the twang, the cadence. Write a biography of your characters, including names, ages, physical descriptions, and personal qualities. Otherwise, in the fourth chapter, twenty-three-year-old Beth, with auburn hair and blue eyes, is twenty-four and brunette; and sweet Kendra is mean and sassy a few chapters later. Know the internal voice and motivation of your characters. Write a backstory for each of them. You don't have to use this in the book, but you need to know what drives them.

TIP from Mary: I'm a pantser. When I wrote my novel, Cock-eyed, I typed away in a dreamy state until the end. The story was great. The characters were interesting. But there turned out to be too many inconsistencies in the details. Which of Samuel's eyes twitched? The left or the right? What was the name of Chief Half Moon's ancestral town? Red River or Guadalupe? Did Jake say "y'all" or "all y'all"? How old was Avani when he first met Lizzy? Did the diamonds have a yellowish cast or were they as clear as glass? Yikes!

The group was confused. I was confused. I found myself shuffling and swiping back through chapters to find my answers. I began to start lists of character traits, dates, places, dialect, etc. I wish I had figured out from the start that I needed to be doing that.

Keeping track of data is more than important. It's crucial. Without consistency and continuity, your story is an imperfectly beaten soufflé, collapsing the moment you take it out of the oven. BE PREPARED!

TIP from Claire: Keep alphabetical folders (online or paper) on main characters, so you can pull one out quickly when you need to get a fact or add a fact.

- **Set the scene** by giving enough (but not too much) detail as to where and when your character's actions are taking place.
  - Reestablish the scene frequently in each chapter.
    - » You can mention something in the setting.
    - » You can mention an action or movement of the protagonist.
    - » You can refer to the day or the year.
- **Refresh the reader** to relevant points in every chapter.
- **Use foreshadowing** throughout the book. You should drop a hint, plant a seed, in the first chapter that portends what going to happen. Then continue with seeding little nuggets throughout the story. It's okay if at the end of the first draft, you go back in the story to do this.
- **Move the story forward**. Anton Chekhov said that nothing should be included in one's writing that is not necessary to tell the story. I'm sure you've heard his alluding to a gun—if there is a gun hanging over the fireplace in scene one, it must be used in the next one or two scenes. Nothing extraneous to the story should be included in your writing. It's often referred to as "the smoking gun." If it's there, you know it's coming into play. Does what you're writing move the story forward? If not . . . it doesn't belong there, no matter how interesting it is to you. Throw out those sentences you agonized over to make perfect, or the metaphor you just have to use. Sometimes your favorite metaphor, or line of prose, or even an entire chapter may need to go, because it no longer moves the story forward. Save it in a separate file. It may come in handy in some later project.

TIP from Claire: Removing a favorite gem in which I've invested a lot of time can be agonizing. But once it's done, I feel free. I used to spend hours (embarrassing fact) trying to keep in a line I thought was fantastic. When I eventually stopped trying, I would save it in a Word Doc titled "Gems." But I've never gone back and used one! It's best just to move on! Kinda like breaking up with a long-time boyfriend who's just not Mr. Right.

- **Leave the reader wondering what comes next.** What questions can you leave the reader with so they keep on reading?

> *TIP from Mary:* Keep on reading *is a mantra all writers whisper to themselves as they sign off on each chapter. Authors want their readers to miss their eleven o'clock bedtimes and not put their books down. How do you, as an author, do that? How do you leave your readers with a hunger to know what happens next? Nail them with a powerful last line. Example: A long, silver safe-deposit key landed on the Formica counter with a* plink. *Beside it was a business card from a local bank, with Charlotte's distinctive handwriting on it that read: IMPORTANT!*

- **Come full circle in the story.** Don't leave any loose ends (unless you're intentionally doing so in a series, for example.)
- **Polish** your opening and closing lines for the book as well as for each chapter.

> *TIP from Mary: When I first began writing my novel, I never considered tracking questions that needed to be answered. My intent was to write a book with stand-alone short stories that would ultimately converge with a* big bang *ending. My initial draft seemed fine, for none of my first readers waved any warning flags. Closer examination, however, revealed I neglected to tie up all the loose ends. Not the big ones—okay, maybe one—but many of the lesser ones. The bottom line, your readers cannot be left wondering what happened to Aunt Jane, or the ruby ring left in her jewelry box. During the editing process, I now download each chapter, read it, take a red pen and keep a running list of questions that need to be answered.*

- **Read a lot** and observe different authors' writing styles. Reading good writing will influence your own writing.
- **Ideas** expire: be sure to **jot your ideas down** before they disappear.

The Whole Is Greater Than the Sum of Its Parts

Does this all sound overwhelming? Well, it can be. But the good news is that as Aristotle said, the synergy that happens in a group makes everything happen with greater ease. You'll have kindred spirits along for the ride as you navigate this new terrain. There is always one person in our group who understands a concept and can break it down into layperson terms for the rest of us. Plus, we have one another's backs. We keep each other on track. It's so much easier to see where someone has veered off the path when it's not your own work. For us, it's a win-win situation to be in a writing group; we are both student and teacher.

In the next chapters I will go into more detail about what we have learned as a group in terms of building our writing and our editing skills. The two go hand in hand. I will share with you what has worked for us in developing the story, writing with more grace, keeping the story moving forward, and other key elements in the creative process.

CHAPTER SEVEN
Show and *Tell*

Don't tell me the moon is shining;
show me the glint of light on broken glass.
—Anton Chekhov

In writing, it is necessary to both *show* and *tell*. *Telling*, in writing, is necessary in terms of establishing the backstory, setting the scene, or moving the story forward. *Telling* is an important component of a story, fiction or nonfiction. But if your story is only *telling*, your writing will be rather bland. What gives a story color and texture, what draws in the reader is *showing*.

Telling

Don't start your story with page after page of information that you are sure the reader needs to know right away. This is known as an *info dump* and will bore your readers. I guarantee it. Weave the background story into the first few chapters in such a way that the reader absorbs what they need to know as they are being introduced to your protagonist and the scintillating situation they find themselves in. Don't overwhelm them with a lot of detail. Some *telling* is necessary to set the scene, give the backstory, and move the story forward, but be judicious in how you present it. Less is more.

Jump right into the middle of the action. You will grab your readers' attention that way. Which leads us right to *showing*.

Showing

Showing is evocative and expressive. *Showing* allows your readers to experience the story through their senses; they can see it, they can hear it, they can feel it, they can smell it, they can taste it, they can touch it. It evokes an emotional response to the character or the action. *Showing* can be done in many ways. Following are some of the mechanics of *showing* taken from our writing group.

- **Use strong specific verbs**.
  - Lizzy demanded the diamonds be handed over immediately.
    Not: Lizzy asked him to give her the diamonds.
  - Georgiana crushed a scented handkerchief to her nose each time the horses lumbered through town.
    Not: Georgiana didn't like the smell of the passing horses when they came through town.
- **Avoid overusing adverbs**.
  - With a skip in her step, Hannah ran toward her mother.
    Not: Hannah ran happily toward her mother.
  - "You . . . better . . . never . . . do . . . that . . . again . . . Hannah. Or else . . .." her mother said.
    Not: "Don't do that again," her mother said threateningly.
- **Use expressive dialogue to show characters' emotions and attitudes.**
  - "Are you nuts? I'm not touching that," Pat says, a look of horror stealing across her face.
    "What are we gonna do? This is crazy," I say, as I wrap my arms around my torso, trying to stop the shivering despite the warmth of the day. "This is really a dead guy, isn't it?" I'm praying she'll disagree with me, as my eyes are drawn to the bottom of his leg where there should be a foot, but instead is a mangled stump.
    Not: Pab told me that she wouldn't touch the body. I was cold and wondered if it was really a dead person. I kept looking at the mangled stump of his leg.
- **Use words that embody the moment**.
  - The late-afternoon fall sun warmed me as I read in front of the bay window.
    Not: I sat in front of the sunny window reading.
  - Laughter carried across the long expanse of green grass, as the newly-married couple posed outside the sun-drenched church for their wedding pictures.
    Not: They laughed while they were having their wedding pictures taken.

- **Show the effect of speech on the speaker but avoid using speech tags**. A basic speech tag (a noun and verb delineating who is speaking) is necessary in writing but, ideally, should be kept as invisible as possible so the reader can forget they are reading. Sometimes adding an adverb helps give the reader an idea of what the speaker is experiencing, but in general it works best to *show* what they are experiencing.
  - She held her head high with only a hint of trepidation in her voice as she said, "Mr. Gillis, I want a raise."
    Not: "Can I have a raise, Mr. Gillis," she said nervously.
  - Running alongside his daughter as she rode her bike for the first time without training wheels, his breath came in short gasps and his forehead glistened with sweat, as he said, "Great job, Eva. Keep on going."
    Not: "Great job, Eva. Keep on going," he said out of breath.
- **Engage the reader through descriptions of actions, movements, and appearances**.
  - When your brain is working well, you may find you swagger your hubris with spunk and accomplish what you set out to do—clarity of thought brings about clarity of action!
    Not: You will get more done when your brain is working well.
  - Jake's mouth dropped open as he watched Samuel bolt for the car.
    Not: He watched Samuel run to the car and was shocked.
- **Use active words and expressions**.
  - I continued to scrutinize and scour, to rummage and forage, to look high and low, to examine the mainstream and delve into the obscure.
    Not: I kept looking for information.
  - Before feasting on the array of facts that follow, nibble on this dauntingly impactful one.
    Not: This is important.
  - She squinted, scrunched her nose, and burned a hole straight through me.
    Not: She stared at me.

- **Use sensory words that evoke sight, sound, feeling, smell, taste, and touch**.
    - Astonishment was aglow in my brain. A row of windows framing a blue sky elevated the sparkling moment.
    Not: This was interesting to me.
    - My head ached, my stomach knotted, and a bitter taste captured my tongue as I pushed those thoughts away.
    Not: I felt bad.

Use metaphors.
    - He was drowning in a sea of grief.
    Not: He was terribly sad.
    - She could smell the stench of failure stalking her.
    Not: She was afraid she would fail.
    - Super Foods are Super Heroes with Super Powers—like antioxidants—which destroy super villains, free radicals.
    Not: Super Foods contain antioxidants that fight off free radicals.
    - A broke horse, I surrendered and trotted back without a word.
    Not: I gave up.

By employing these techniques in your writing, you evoke the physical and emotional experience of the characters. The reader will feel as if they're in the story. They'll believe the story. And by not *telling* them what to think or feel, you allow them to draw their own conclusions.

There's no right amount of *show* and *tell* to include in your book. Some writers use very little show. However, in most books, fiction and nonfiction alike, you'll see a well-choreographed dance between *show* and *tell*. For most new writers, it is a talent that needs to be honed. Just as it's essential for a dancer to do hundreds of practice pirouettes and arabesques before she opens as Clara in "The Nutcracker Suite," it's essential to write hundreds of practice scenes before you write that *New York Times* bestseller.

Show-It Short Story

✓ **Practice *show***
✓ **Prep: Yes**

Purpose: This exercise is designed to practice the technique of *showing* to give your readers free rein to experience the story through their senses; they can see it, they can hear it, they can feel it, they can smell it, they can taste it, they can touch it. *Showing* evokes an emotional response to the character or to the action. (Our group did this exercise every week for months to hone our *showing* skills.)

Prep: One week prior to meeting: One member chooses a photograph and emails it to the group members. The picture can be anything—a country scene, a city scene, a silly scene; it can contain people or animals, or not.

Prep: Individual instructions prior to the group meeting: Write a short story using the setting in the chosen photograph you have received as the backdrop for a character's reaction to a situation they are in.

1. Write a one- to two-page, double-spaced story based on the photograph.
2. Write the story from the perspective of a dangerous person, a nervous person, a monk, or your protagonist.
3. While some *tell* will be necessary in your story, focus on using techniques you've learned for *showing* the scene and the character(s).
4. Have at least one to three characters.
5. Create a story line with a beginning, middle, and end.
6. Title your story.

Group instructions for the meeting:

1. Each member gives hard copies of their story to the group members.
2. Each member reads their story aloud.
3. After each reading, the group provides feedback as to what worked, what didn't work, what was *show* and what was *tell*, and discusses other techniques the author might consider.
4. Discuss the similarities and differences in the individual approaches taken for the same photograph.

Group critique:

1. Did the author evoke the physical and emotional experience of the character(s)?
2. Did the author use sensory words, active verbs, and expressions? Metaphors?
3. Did the author use dialogue?
4. Did the author use words that embody the moment?
5. Most of all, did the author engage you, the reader?

CHAPTER EIGHT

Going Deeper with Metaphors and Similes

The story has to move down, as well as forward.
—Rachel Basch

None of us could imagine having the same success without one another's encouragement to **move the story forward**, a key element in storytelling. But besides forward movement, a writer must also move the story deeper. We are always on the lookout for opportunities to bring more depth to our stories. One thing we do as we are editing is to look for places where a **metaphor** or a **simile** would enhance someone's writing.

People use metaphors every day without even thinking about it. It was raining cats and dogs yesterday. (This comes from medieval England when homes had thatched roofs and family dogs and cats would sleep on the roof to stay warm. In heavy rains, the thatch would cave in; ergo it was raining cats and dogs.) My skin was crawling. It's hot as Hades out. She was as limp as a dishrag. And on and on and on. Most of these would fall under the category of "dead" metaphors, as they've been overused and are quite outdated. But we know what they mean; we can hear the heavy downpour outside, feel bugs crawling on our arms, experience the unbearable heat and humidity, or visualize a woman who can barely stand up. Which is the point of a metaphor.

Metaphors

A **metaphor** is "a figure of speech in which a word or phrase literally denoting one kind of object or idea is used in place of another to suggest a likeness . . . between them (as in *drowning in money*)." *Merriam-Webster.com Dictionary*, s.v. "metaphor," accessed March 24, 2021, https://www.merriam-webster.com/dictionary/metaphor.

A metaphor helps the reader *experience* the written word. It evokes a vision using a completely different set of images than would normally be associated with the word or phrase. Here are examples from our own work:

- Samuel shed his skin as he slithered into his next dubious venture.
  Not: Samuel was a con man.

- Ulysses was the metronome of Moodus.
  Not: Ulysses founded the Drum and Fife Corp, led an orchestra, and supported the music hall in his hometown of Moodus.
- Lizzie is the crack in the firecracker.
  Not: Lizzie has energy.
- Hannah's life had more pitfalls than Chutes and Ladders.
  Not: Hannah's life was full of ups and downs.
- A pregnant woman is Atlas shouldering the world with her breasts and a womb.
  Not: Pregnant women have a lot of responsibilities.

There are two ways to use metaphors in storytelling. Firstly, a writer can use a metaphor to bring color and texture and depth to their story. Metaphors delight the reader by expanding their experience. Secondly, characters can use metaphors in dialogue. Both enrich your story. In Shoreline Writers, when we're writing scenes and descriptions, we want our metaphors to be original. We want to make sure it is appropriate to the era in which our story takes place. If we're writing about a trip to New York City in the 1880s, to say, "Let's go to the Big Apple" would not make sense. And we want to only use our metaphor once.

On the other hand, to use an old, outdated, "dead metaphor" in 2020 is equally not appropriate. For example, here are some metaphors people used to describe older folks:

- has one foot in the grave
- is getting long in the tooth
- is no spring chicken

These are antiquated, dead metaphors, also known as clichés. Avoid using dead metaphors as they no longer hold any oomph, even though they may still be implicitly understood. But, as mentioned above, if you're writing about the era out of which the metaphor arose, they may be appropriate, especially if your character is using them in dialogue.

Another trap to avoid is using a "mixed metaphor." A mixed metaphor is comprised of parts of two or more metaphors which don't belong together. *A bad penny can spoil the bunch* is a mixed metaphor combining the two metaphors: *They keep turning up like a bad penny* and *One bad apple can spoil the bunch.* Here are the origins of these two very dead metaphors. The first comes from the mid-eighteenth century when pennies were valuable and often counterfeited. You might find yourself with a bad penny in your pocket, spend it quickly with an unsuspecting grocer, then get it back in change the next time you shopped. The second refers to the fact that one rotting apple can cause the whole barrel of apples to rot. Both of these examples are old, outdated metaphors and probably not the best choice of ones to use, even if you keep them straight.

The last mistake to be on the lookout for is using a metaphor that does not fit the story. For example, if someone is writing about the Wild West, they should use metaphors about cowpokes and mustangs and campfires and wagon trains. They should not use metaphors about islands in the South Pacific or snowboarding or sushi or rocket ships. They'll stick out like a sore thumb (sorry!). Stay in your world!

Similes

A **simile** is "a figure of speech comparing two unlike things that is often introduced by *like* or *as* (as in *cheeks like roses)."* "Simile." *Merriam-Webster.com Dictionary*, Merriam-Webster, https://www.merriam-webster.com/dictionary/simile. Accessed 24 Mar. 2021.

Similes can be simple comparisons: She was as honest as the day was long. He is as sly as a fox.

Or they can be complex, as Charles Dickens wrote in *David Copperfield*, describing Dora's cousin: ". . . with such long legs that he looked like the afternoon shadow of somebody else."

As with metaphors, we all use similes in our everyday conversation. *I'm as tired as all get out. She's as cool as a cucumber. Her hair looked like a waterfall cascading down her back.* The difference is that similes will have the comparison words "as" or "like" in them.

Similes are not as powerful as metaphors. A metaphor is a punch, while a simile is like a little push. Which paints a stronger picture? You'll decide based on what you're writing.

> All the world's a stage,
> And all the men and women merely players;
> They have their exits and their entrances . . .
> —William Shakespeare, *As You Like It*

"Metaphors" by Sylvia Plath

✓ **Explore using metaphors as a means of** *showing*
✓ **Prep: Yes**

Purpose: This exercise is designed to explore the power of metaphors to bring a story to life.

Prep: Individual instructions prior to the group meeting: Read and answer questions about the poem "Metaphors" by Sylvia Plath.

1. Read "Metaphors" by Sylvia Plath. (The poem can be found online or in Ed Hughes, ed., *Sylvia Plath: The Collected Poems.* New York: Harper Perennial, 2016.)
2. Answer the following questions:
   • What is the poem about?
   • Which metaphor is easiest to understand? Why?
   • Which metaphor is hardest to understand? Why?
   • Which metaphor created the best imagery in your mind? Why?
   • Which metaphor sparked the highest emotion in you? Why?
   • What would the author be saying if she didn't use metaphors, i.e. what is her message?
   • How many metaphors can you find? Hint: There are more than meet the eye.

Materials for group: Each member brings a copy of the poem and their answers to the questions.

Group instructions for the meeting:
1. One member reads the poem aloud.
2. Discuss the poem using the answers to the questions above as a jumping off place.

Create Your Own Metaphors

✓ **Create metaphors as a means of *showing***
✓ **Prep: Yes**

Purpose: This exercise is designed to practice writing metaphors.

Prep: Individual instructions prior to the group meeting: Write new metaphors to replace this well-worn one: My life is such a roller coaster. Refer to the following instructions and examples to complete this exercise. Don't worry if your metaphors are basic or cliché. You're doing this to get the idea of how to write metaphors.

	INSTRUCTIONS	EXAMPLE
1.	Write a sentence using the rollercoaster metaphor.	"Since I lost my job, my life has been a rollercoaster."
2.	Rewrite the sentence describing the sensations you are trying to convey with the words "rollercoaster."	"Since I lost my job, I've had a series of abrupt ups and downs, starts and stops."

3.	A rollercoaster is only one way to convey the sensation of many abrupt changes. There are other worlds besides the amusement park world where abrupt, frequent, and unexpected changes happen. Take the natural world for example. Try to complete this sentence using a metaphor from the sea world: "Since I lost my job, I have been . . ."	From the natural world: "Since I lost my job, I've been tossed about on the sea of rejection with the ever present threat of creatures unseen and no life raft in sight."
4.	Choose other worlds. (Ideas: vehicles, food, technology, art etc.) You might want to start with a simile, then remove the "like" or "as" to form a metaphor.	From the *food world*, a simile: 1. "Since I lost my job, I'm like a potato in a whirling food processor trying to dodge the killer blades." 2. "Since I lost my job, my brain is like a whirling food processor, chopping, blending, and pureeing every thought I have." Changed to a metaphor: 1. "Since I lost my job, I'm a potato in a whirling food processor trying to dodge the killer blades." 2. Since I lost my job, my brain is a whirling food processor, chopping, blending, and pureeing every thought I have."

Materials for group: Each member brings copies of their metaphors for the group.

Group instructions for the meeting:
1. Each member reads their metaphor and discusses how it evolved.
2. Brainstorm metaphors to describe one another.
   - Here's one of our examples: Mary Virginia is the crack in the firecracker.

CHAPTER NINE
Wordsmithing with Flair

The difference between the almost right word and the right word is …
the difference between the lightning bug and the lightning.
—Mark Twain

The process of discovering those right words and organizing them into a cohesive sentence that morphs into a well-structured paragraph requires practice. (Unless you're one of those genius writers we talked about earlier.) At Shoreline Writers, we focus a great deal on helping one another with wordsmithing. And we do that by studying established writers.

We have found that we learn best from those who have walked this path before, succeeded, and shared their wisdom. In this chapter, we will share four writing techniques that we have found helpful to do as a group. A technique that may not make sense when first read, is clarified under the scrutiny of multiple sets of eyes. Getting advice from one another on how to approach these exercises has helped each of us evolve in our writing.

Wordsmithing Technique #1
Psychic Distance

The first wordsmithing concept is John Gardner's notion of "psychic distance." As he explains in *The Art of Fiction*, psychic distance refers to the gap readers feel between themselves and the events and characters in the story. As you read the description of the levels of psychic distance which follows, imagine you are looking through the lens of a telescope and able to zoom in closer to the scene and character at each level. When you use this lens to focus in more closely, you see the details of the story more clearly, which allows you to enter the magic of the written world.

The five levels of psychic distance are:
- **Level One** is distant and objective; it grounds the reader in time and place. (*No zoom*)

- **Level Two** begins to bring in personal information within the setting. (*Slight zoom*)
- **Level Three** allows the character to emerge while the narrator is still in control. (*Slightly more zoom*)
- **Level Four** goes deeper into a character's thoughts and POV. (*Even greater zoom*)
- **Level Five** brings out the character's voice fully; the narrator disappears. This is where you find yourself fully immersed in the story! (*Full zoom*)

Some scenes may incorporate all five levels, drawing closer to the character and setting as the lens adjusts from Level One to Level Five. This telescoping technique allows the writer to deliver whatever background material they think necessary (Level One into Level Two). But the more characters live at Level Five, the more rewarding it is for the reader. It is not necessary to use all five levels. But it is necessary to determine at what level you should write at any given time. This is a fluid process, and one that necessitates continuous adjustment of the lens based on how far away, or close, the author wants their readers to be to the story.

Following are examples of psychic distance from our own works-in-progress.

Mary:
Level One: Her mother had a secret.
Level Two: Lizzy Lombardo knew little about her mother's past.
Level Three: Lizzy swore she'd uncover her mother's secrets.
Level Four: Damn, how she hated all the lies and not knowing the truth.
Level Five: She clenched her fists in anger. She'd never met her relatives. Never seen their photographs. And hell, she'd never even been to Texas.

In **Level One**, the narrator tells the reader that someone's mother has a secret. There is *no zoom*.

In **Level Two**, the narrator tells us the name of the character, Lizzy Lombardo. This *slight zoom* still keeps the psychic distance.

In **Level Three**, the narrator brings the reader into Lizzy's head and lets them know something personal about the character. She hated the lies. There is *slightly more zoom.*

In **Level Four**, the reader is brought deeper into the character's thoughts and feelings. There is *even greater zoom.*

In **Level Five**, the reader is fully immersed in Lizzy's experience. Their senses are engaged by her emotional state. Readers can relate to their own experiences in situations like this. Psychic distance dissolves as the telescope is adjusted to *full zoom.*

Now apply the same principles to the following examples.

Debbie:
  Level One: She saw something on the beach.
  Level Two: The young girl didn't know what she was looking at.
  Level Three: Hannah couldn't believe it. Could it be possible?
  Level Four: No way. It can't be. Is that a body?
  Level Five: Oh my god. It's a dead body. It's so black . . . and bloated. What do I do? Oh, no. This is horrible.

Claire:
  Level One: At the courthouse in Middletown, a lady sat in the gallery.
  Level Two: Sitting straight and motionless, Georgiana stared at her brother on the stand.
  Level Three: When she tried to give him a supportive smile, her face wouldn't obey.
  Level Four: With her handkerchief snarled in her hands, she avoided dabbing her pooled eyes, and instead, lifted her head high to keep tears from spilling onto her satin bodice for all, including him, to see.
  Level Five: Her insides were bruised from the year-long fight between old pride and new shame, between sympathy and disgust, and between hope and despair, but love for her brother had no competition.

Dianne:

Level One: The brain. Ponder its magnificence.

Level Two: I'd like to think our bodies—organs, muscles, bones and nerves—instinctively recognize the nobility of the brain.

Level Three: Of all the organs performing dazzling feats—the heart beats 115,000 times a day, the lungs deliver oxygen and expel carbon dioxide, the intricate vascular network is almost beyond comprehension—one stands out from the rest. The brain.

Level Four: Perhaps they laud the dignity and brilliance of the brain because they know the brain runs the show. When the breath flutters with passion, the heart warms with love or the nerves interpret tenderness, they can only do so because the brain is directing them to do so.

Level Five: The brain is the most precious, precocious and cherished organ. Its value is beyond measure. It cannot be replaced or transplanted; it must be honored and looked up to. Perhaps the brain's positioning is intentional, distinguishing itself with the requirement that we look up to it!

Psychic Distance

✓ Less *tell,* more *show*
✓ Prep: Yes

Purpose: This exercise, based on John Gardner's technique of "psychic distance," is designed to help the writer focus in, like a telescope zooming closer and closer, and narrow the distance between the narrator and the character/scene. More distance equals more *tell.* Less distance equals more *show.*

Prep: Individual instructions prior to the group meeting: Apply Gardner's five stages of psychic distance to a scene and take the reader from the narrator's voice into the character's head and the scene, lessening the *tell* and increasing the *show.* This exercise gives you practice in writing from the perspective of the different levels of psychic distance. You will then be able to pick and choose what level(s) you wish to use in your work. Normally, you would not include all five levels in one setting.

1. Modify a passage from your writing or create a new one, then write a scene that includes all five of the levels of psychic distance listed. Label each level.

    - **Level One** is distant and objective; it grounds the reader in time and place. (No zoom)
    - **Level Two** begins to bring in personal information within the setting. (Slight zoom)
    - **Level Three** allows the character to emerge while the narrator is still in control. (Slightly greater zoom)
    - **Level Four** goes deeper into a character's thoughts and point of view. (Even greater zoom)
    - **Level Five** brings out the character's voice fully, while the narrator disappears. (Full zoom)

Materials for group: Each member brings copies of their scene and the **Five Levels** listed above.

Group instructions for the meeting:
1. Each member reads their writing aloud.
2. After each reader, the group discusses whether the objective has been met.

Group critique:
1. Using the template for psychic distance, discuss how the writer has decreased the psychic distance between the reader and the narrator from a Level One to a Level Five.
2. Discuss the methods used.
3. If not successful at closing the psychic distance, what might they have done differently?
4. What was each member's experience of this writing exercise?

Wordsmithing Technique #2
The Tip of the Iceberg

If a writer of prose knows enough of what he is writing about he may omit things that he knows and the reader, if the writer is writing truly enough, will have a feeling of those things as strongly as though the writer had stated them. The dignity of movement of an ice-berg is due to only one-eighth of it being above water. A writer who omits things because he does not know them only makes hollow places in his writing.

—Ernest Hemingway in *Death in the Afternoon*

After discovering Hemingway's Tip of the Iceberg theory during one of our retreats, our group devoted time to understanding and practicing this literary giant's technique. This was another opportunity for us to work on *show* and *tell*, which this technique personifies. Hemingway does not tell his reader what to see, what to hear, or what to feel. Instead, he creates a world in which these senses are brought to life.

We began by reading Hemingway's short story "The Big Two-Hearted River," which is based on Hemingway's own experiences in World War I. His protagonist Nick goes on a backwoods fishing trip. The story has a multitude of references to fire: hills of burnt timber; burned over country; split by fire; the surface . . . burned off the ground; burned over stretch of hillside; the burned town; the high, fire-scarred hill. Later he notices grasshoppers with their armor blackened and wonders if they will always be black because of the fire.

The story is a metaphor for war. Yet nowhere in the story docs Hemingway mention that Nick has been in the war. However, it is clear from what he has written that Nick has been impacted by trauma. From the timeframe of the story, it is clear it was World War I.

Hemingway believed that a writer could convey the meaning of the story while writing about something seemingly irrelevant to the topic. What, one might wonder, do blackened grasshoppers have to do with war? Nothing directly, but it is not a far stretch of the imagination to picture armies marching off to places unknown and facing perils along the way. And in fact, his story is made all the more powerful because of what is left to the reader's imagination.

At Shoreline Writers, we try to incorporate the Tip of the Iceberg theory into our writing. This is one reason we do research into our subject matter, and why we stress the importance of doing this before you begin your book. Know enough about your subject matter to fill the mass of the iceberg that is underwater. Use symbolism, metaphors, and other descriptive techniques that allow the reader to discover for themselves the meaning hidden below the surface.

Tip of the Iceberg

✓ **Practice** *show*
✓ **Prep: Yes**

Purpose: This exercise is designed to practice *show*. Use Hemingway's Tip of the Iceberg theory, which states that if you know your subject well enough you can omit obvious details; and if you write it well enough, the reader will implicitly understand what the story is about.

Prep: Individual instructions prior to the group meeting: Write a short story without telling the reader who the main character is or telling them what has happened.

1. Read Hemingway's short story "The Big Two-Hearted River."
2. Write a one- to two-page short story using one of the following scenes:
   - An old woman is walking on a path by a lake. Her husband, a mean and abusive man, has just died.
   - A young man is walking on a busy street in a city. He has just committed murder.
   - A father who encouraged his daughter to continue the family tradition of joining the military has just been informed by two army representatives that she was killed in the line of duty. He sits on the porch watching them drive away.
   - A woman steals a diamond necklace from a jewelry display at Neiman Marcus. The jewelry section is on the fourth floor, and she is leaving the building.
   - A teenager causes an accident while texting and driving. He narrowly avoids hitting a bicyclist who swerves out of his way but directly into the path of an oncoming vehicle. The teenager does not stop and drives home.

3. Use what you've learned about the Tip of the Iceberg theory to write your story without revealing who the character is or revealing what has happened.
4. Make hard copies for your group.

Materials for group: Each member brings copies of their short story.

Group instructions for the meeting:
1. Each member shares a hard copy of their story with the group.
2. Each member reads their story aloud.
3. The group provides feedback as to what worked, didn't work, and other possibilities the author might explore.

Group critique:
1. How did the author evoke the physical and emotional experiences of the character?
2. Has the author used sensory words? Active verbs and expressions? Metaphors?
3. Has the author used dialogue?
4. Most of all, has the author engaged you, the reader?

Wordsmithing Technique #3
The Camera Test

When we're critiquing one another's work, we often ask the writer what she sees in her head to assess if it matches the image she's presented on the page. If it doesn't, we'll work with her to get more of it down on paper, so we, as readers, can fully grasp what she has intended. It's easy to have a perfectly clear image in your mind and assume the reader can see it. Getting everything down on paper is not as easy to do as it might seem to be, but with a group critique, there's always another opportunity to work at it.

In his book, *The First 50 Pages*, Jeff Gerke describes a simple, but practical technique to help writers focus on whether there is enough *show* and *tell* for the reader to fully see the character/scene. His premise? He suggests you look at a scene and ask yourself, "Can the camera see it?" Imagine you are filming a movie; what would the scene look like? This approach will help you focus on getting down on the page exactly what is in your mind. This was one of the first techniques we tackled in our group.

Read the following passage:

The beach was practically empty. A few solitary walkers combed the shore, avoiding the waves and each other. The gulls circled overhead, occasionally dropping into the rough waters to fish. Lily saw none of this.

What did you experience reading this? Now look at it through the camera's eye. What can the camera see? Perhaps you can visualize the beach and the walkers and the gulls, but can you feel the experience of those beach walkers? Can you picture what they are feeling? No, you can't. This paragraph is simply *telling* the reader what is happening. *Telling* alone can be quite boring, as this paragraph is. Does it make you want to keep reading?

Now read this:

As the dark clouds rolled in, the waves hit the shore with such fierceness that the few determined walkers who'd ventured down to the shore on this blustery morning were forced to flee further up the beach. Lily pulled her wool hat lower on her forehead and struggled to gain control of her scarf, the wind whipping the fringed edges across her face. Herring gulls fought the air currents as they circled and dipped into the frothy waves, their wings attempting to maintain a steady path toward their next meal. With downward cast eyes, Lily took in nothing but the swirling sand beneath her feet. It fit her mood perfectly.

What's your response to this paragraph? Can the camera see this? Yes! While there is not much action, you get a clear and succinct description of both the beach and Lily's reaction to being on it. We can relate to walking on a beach in the winter with the wind blowing so hard you can barely see where you are going. You move inside Lily's head in this paragraph and see and feel what she sees and feels.

This writing uses description to bring us into the setting of the story, which is *show*. Setting, as we've discussed, is crucial to the story, as much as character and plot are. If the camera can see what the author has written, the reader can see it as well.

While there are exceptions to what the camera can see, such as taste, smell, temperature, sound, and inner dialogue (and where aren't there exceptions in writing guidelines?), there are ways you can show these sensory experiences. Lily wraps her coat tightly around her body (temperature); Lily sniffs the air (smell); Lily grimaces as she bites into her apple (taste). The portrayal of nonvisual concepts may take a little more work, but if the camera can capture it, the reader will as well.

Can the Camera See It?

✓ **Practice** *show*
✓ **Prep: Yes**

Purpose: This exercise is designed to further finesse the concept of *showing*. This approach will help you focus on getting down on the page exactly what you see in your mind.

Prep: Individual instructions prior to the group meeting: Take a scene from your writing and rewrite it while imagining you are filming a movie. Ask yourself the question: Can the camera see it?
1. Choose a sample of your writing (one scene) or create a new scene.
2. Write the scene through the lens of the camera. What can the camera see?
3. Make copies for the group.

Materials for group: Each member brings copies of their writing for the group.

Group instructions for the meeting:
1. Each member reads their scene aloud.
2. The group discusses whether the camera can see it.

Group critique:
1. Did the author create a picture in your mind?
2. Do you think the author is showing or telling?
3. Can you feel what the author is saying?
4. Did the author clearly present the setting? Character? Scene?
5. Has the author fully revealed what's in their imagination?
   • Ask the author if there is more to what they were visualizing than made it into the story.

Wordsmithing Technique #4
Layering

Much has been written about the concept of layering in writing. It's like painting: you layer on the paint to get the look and feel that you want. Some writers layer as they go, others go back to add in layers. Whichever way you do it, the goal of layering is to add depth and dimension to your writing. It's not about merely adding to your word count, it's about painting a picture through your words that tells the story. It's the seven-layer cake vs. the sheet cake. There's way more frosting in every piece.

According to Rebecca Zanetti () there are seven opportunities to add a layer to your story: dialogue, action, reaction, emotions, senses, setting/atmosphere, and backstory. Rebecca Zanetti, accessed March 23, 2021, https://rebeccazanetti.com/writing-craft/1745-2/

1. Dialogue: Both what your dialogue says and doesn't say is important. What is the tone of your character's voice? Her choice of words? Her attitude? Is he a strong, silent type? Is he quiet and unassuming? Is she tough as nails with the vocabulary of a sailor? But dialogue alone isn't enough. It needs dimensionality.

2. Action: Action supplements both dialogue and silence, imbuing the scene with different meanings depending on what else the character is doing. What is your protagonist up to while she's sitting on the train, heading to her mother's funeral from whom she's been estranged for the last five years? Is she pensively staring out the window? Is she furiously scribbling in her journal? Is she on her cell phone, playing games, checking Facebook, texting friends? Is she pulling out her eyelashes? Tattooing herself with her Bic pen?

3. Reaction: How your character reacts in situations and to other people will define her. Does she always have an edge? Is she timid or tough? A smart aleck or reserved? Does she take charge or follow the crowd? Is she prone to anger or prone to crying? Is she a bully? Is she a tightwad? Is she a volcano about ready to erupt?

4. Emotions: Emotions can be simple and straightforward or complex and hidden. Mad, sad, glad, and scared are the four primary feelings, but how many variations on the theme can you come up with? How does your protagonist react emotionally in different situations? Is she predictable or is she always full of surprises? Does she cry when she's angry? Yell when she's sad? Hold in her feelings?

5. Senses: Let your character utilize all her senses as a device to show her relationship with her environment. What smells does she notice? Does perfume make her sneeze? Does the smell of lilacs remind her of her grandmother? What does she hear in the background as she's walking around the estate, looking for clues as to what happened to the missing wife? What does she feel as she blindly gropes her way out of the cave? What is it like when she emerges from the dark and is greeted by the blinding flashlight of her rescuer shining in her eyes? What memories are stirred up by the taste of cotton candy at the county fair?

6. Setting/Atmosphere: Describe the setting from your character's point of view. Men, women, children, adults, gamers, bibliophiles, introverts, extroverts, Americans traveling abroad, foreigners visiting America will see something different in their surroundings that will orient the reader to their personality and their world perspective.

7. Backstory: As you can see from these examples, the character's backstory is interwoven with the layering in of the senses, setting, emotions, actions, reactions, and dialogue. This all works in harmony to bring depth to the characters and the plot, so that the reader becomes completely immersed in the story, a great indicator of a well-written book.

TIP from Claire: Sometimes the layer comes first.

Sometimes you find the layer before your story is fully developed. Sometimes a potential layer inspires a new angle. I find myself collecting nuggets that I might use later for layering. For example, in searching through nineteenth-century newspapers for

---

a mention of my character's name, I saw several advertisements for corsets. That led me to capture some descriptive words from the ads, which then led me to using the corset as a metaphor for the tight-laced time of my character.

You can collect potential layering points for nonfiction or fiction. I don't worry about organizing them in any particular way, but I do source them. For me, spotting fascinating tidbits, some of which have nothing to do with my story, is fun. Reading them occasionally during the writing process often gives me new inspirations.

Layering Your Story

✓ **Add depth and dimension to your writing**
✓ **Prep: No**

Purpose: This exercise, based on Rebecca Zanetti's description of layering, is designed to help you develop the art of adding depth and dimension to your writing. The purpose is to expand your story through layering. This facilitates more *show* and less *tell*.

Scene: → Anna and Harry Layering Possibilities ↓	A "I really like Jane," Harry said.	B "You've got to be kidding," Anna said.	C "What's the matter with you? She's perfect!"	D "Yeah, right," Anna said.	E "You're just jealous," Harry said.
Dialogue					
Action					
Reaction					
Emotion					
Senses					
Setting					
Backstory					

Group instructions for the meeting:

1. Read Anna and Harry's lines from A to E in the above chart. That is the basic story. Take a moment and think about how to expand this interaction.
2. As a group start with Box A. Each member will add a layer or two to Box A to develop their own story.
3. Repeat for the other four boxes (B – E), adding one or two layers to each box.
4. Then start with Box A again and add one or two more layers.
5. Repeat for the other four boxes (B – E).
6. Repeat for boxes A-E once more. You should have a finished scene at this point.
7. Note: This is a mix and match process. You do not have to use all the layering possibilities. Layers do not have to be in any particular order. You may find that you're adding a layer to one of your layers. You may want to change Scene A entirely as you develop the story more. There is no right and wrong here. Cross out. Modify.
8. Use the chart above to keep track of what you have done.
9. When rounds are finished, the group critiques.

Group critique:

1. Did the author engage you, the reader?
2. Did the author evoke the physical and emotional experience of the characters?
3. Did the author use sensory words? Active verbs and expressions? Metaphors?
4. Has the author used dialogue? Used words that embody the moment?
5. Which layers were most popular among members?
6. Which layers were seldom used by members?

PART THREE

How a Group Edits and Critiques

Good editing takes patience, perseverance, and perspective. As well as a lot of practice. Malcolm Gladwell, in his 2008 bestselling book *Outliers*, attributes the success of the stars in their fields, such as sports champions and musical virtuosos, to having spent ten thousand hours practicing. That means if you're forty years old and you've spent roughly ten hours a week editing since you graduated high school, you'll be at the top of the pile of editors. Not likely, but don't let that discourage you! You don't need to be on the top, but you need to practice editing. A lot! It is a learned skill, in many ways as demanding as the actual writing process.

When Shoreline Writers began meeting, we didn't have a protocol for editing one another's work: when it would happen, how it would be done, or what we were looking for in terms of editing comments. As we evolved, we noticed what was working and what wasn't and streamlined our process. While it's still a work in progress, here's what we've learned so far. It can be summed up this way: Writing is rewriting and editing and more rewriting and editing and more rewriting and more editing and more rewriting . . .

CHAPTER TEN
Editing and Critiquing One Another's Work

Nothing will work unless you do it.
—Maya Angelou

How and when it happens

We aren't totally *old school*, but we're definitely not *techies*. We use a combination of technology and good, old-fashioned pen and paper. We compose in Word on our computers. We email a copy of our writing to the group. Generally, we print out hard copies to edit. We bring those copies with us to our meetings. Then we go back to our computers to edit our own work before posting the finished chapter on Google Docs. Following are some practical tips we'd like to share with you.

1. Prior to our weekly meeting:
   - We email our writing three days in advance to allow for editing time. Members who have submissions email everyone a copy of their work in a Word Doc.
   - These submissions can be a few pages of a chapter, a whole chapter, an outline for a chapter, or anything you want feedback on.
   - For editing ease:
     - use an easily readable font (e.g. Times or Calibri 12pt)
     - double-space
     - number the pages
   - Use all capital letters in the email's subject line: **YOUR NAME, WRITING FOR MEETING, and the DATE.** Example: DEBBIE WRITING FOR WED 10/3/18. This way your email doesn't get lost in the inbox. We learned the hard way with members missing an email and coming in unprepared.
     - Each member prints a copy of the other members' submissions and edits them at home using a red pen, just like our favorite (or not!) teachers did back in school. Do teachers even do this anymore?

2. At the meeting:
   - Bring edited copies to the meeting.
   - Divvy up the time equally between group members. Depending on how many of us have writing that day, and whether we have other exercises to do, we have forty-five minutes each to read and get feedback.
   - Someone reads their work out loud, and the rest give feedback line-by-line. This works well for us. We can bring the same reworked piece of writing to the group for as many weeks as we feel necessary to get it in the shape we want it. Or until we're sick of reworking it or someone yells *UNCLE*!
3. After the meeting:
   - Once this phase of editing a chapter is complete, and we've taken it as far as we can—*for now, at least*—we post it on Google Docs for a final copy editing.
   - We "share" it with all the members.
   - The author puts the group members' names at the top of her document, and when they finish their Google Docs editing, they highlight their name and leave a comment that they're finished. Another tip we learned from experience. This way the author knows when everyone has finished their edits.

What We Do
WE ARE DEVELOPMENTAL EDITORS.
As developmental editors, we look at the big picture.

1. Does the book meet the criteria for the genre the author is writing in? If for example, it's a thriller, is it suspenseful? Is it high stakes and fast paced? If it's a romance novel, does the protagonist live happily ever after with their love interest? If it's a mystery, is there a dead body, high stakes in terms of solving the crime, and a protagonist who seeks the truth?
2. Is the author writing to her audience? If it's a young adult book, is it written to appeal to young adults, which usually involves writing in the first person and from the perspective of a teenager? Is the language what a teenager would use?

3. Is the storyline consistent? We look for gaps in the story. Are characters consistent? If using a dialect, is it used throughout the story? If the protagonist is a brunette but she shows up as a blond three chapters later, did she have a dye job?
4. Does what is written move the story forward?
5. Does the timeline work? Are there unexplained gaps? You can't have someone die in Chapter One and show up alive in Chapter Seven.
6. Is the dialogue natural and realistic?
7. Does the story make sense? If it doesn't make sense to us, it certainly won't make sense to a reader.

WE ARE COPY EDITORS.

As copy editors we check for readability, consistency, and accuracy.
1. Check grammar, punctuation, and spelling.
2. Check sentence and paragraph structure.
3. Check the accuracy of proper nouns, places, and facts.
4. Check for accuracy in the timeline of the story.
5. Check verb tense consistency and subject-verb compatibility.
6. Check for passive vs. active voice, word omissions, and word repetitions.

WE ARE PROOFREADERS.

As proofreaders, we do one last edit on Google Docs. Proofreading is the final step in the editing process, whether in your group or in the publishing world. Proofreading happens after all the other editing has been completed.

Because we've learned to write at the same time we've learned to edit, there is a lot of overlap. The better we get as writers, the better we edit. And vice versa. While we follow the guidelines listed above for professional editors and proofreaders, we edit a little differently. We blend the elements of developmental editing, copy editing, and proofreading. Our first round of editing is basically a developmental edit, although we will point out egregious grammatical error. But primarily we are looking to see if the story works. The second round is a combination of developmental and copy editing. We look to see if the author has fixed the issues in the story that were identified at the previous meeting, as well as doing basic copy editing. The third round of editing, which is on Google Docs, is to proofread the submission and clean it up. An unintended, but welcome, surprise is how intimately we have come to know one another's voices.

What we look for

We are readers. We know what we like and don't like to read, and whom we consider good authors. We are novice writers. We know what we want to say, but don't necessarily know how to get the words on the pages. So, we are constantly striving to improve our writing skills. When possible, we attend writing conferences and seminars, we read books on the subject, or do research online, which has led to us being better editors. As we learn what to do as writers, we learn what to look for in editing. It has been a learning curve, but over time, editing has become intuitive. We don't sit down with this list in front of us while we edit, but we've put it together for you in hopes it will give you a place to start.

What we look for in the content

- **Scene Setting**: Has the scene been established in every chapter? Do we know who, what, where, when, why, and how?
- **Continuity**: Is the chapter consistent with the previous chapter(s) in terms of weather, time of day, season, place, characters, character descriptions, etcetera?
- **Goals, Motivation, Hurdles**: In fiction, the protagonist must have a goal, motivation to achieve that goal, and hurdles to jump over in order to achieve it.
  - **Goal:** What is the protagonist's goal? Is it made clear to the reader early on?
  - **Motivation**: What is the protagonist's motivation to achieve this goal? All main characters need to be motivated to act as they do.
  - **Hurdles:** What gets in the way of the protagonist achieving their goal?
- **Consistency of Voice**: Are there inconsistent reactions or statements not true to the character? Is the language, metaphor, idiom, jargon appropriate for the voice of the character? Is the

voice of the character appropriate to the time?

- **Clichés**: We watch for clichés and rework them.
- **Point of View**: What is the point of view? Is the POV consistent?
- **Clarity**: We look to enhance clarity; those places where the author has the picture established perfectly in their head but hasn't explained it well enough for the reader to understand. Are there confusing moments, or moments you think need to be clarified? When we have to read a sentence or a paragraph twice, it's a clue that clarity can be improved!
- **Show and Tell**: Is the author *telling* or *showing*? Is it the right thing to be doing at that point? If the author is *telling* too much, could this be an opportunity for wordsmithing using the techniques we've learned?
- **The Hook**: Has the writer hooked us with the story? How? Or why not?
  - Do you want to know more about this character and if so, why?
- **Room for Improvement**: Could the author consider doing something different? Is there a better way to get a point across to the reader? We look for opportunities for great writing, impactful writing, and ways to *show* and *tell* more clearly.
- Are facts presented accurately?
- Is the timeline consistent?
- Is the story readable and comprehendible?
- Are there any omissions that need to be addressed?

What we look for in the mechanics

- Is the word order within sentences correct?
- Is the paragraph structure correct?
- What about those commas? Always a biggie!
- We check for multiple word use, repeating a word in the sentence or paragraph.
- We look for inconsistencies or repetitions in what the character or the narrator says.
- Are there misspellings or typos?
- Is the author consistent with tense?

- How's their grammar?
  - Subject-verb compatibility
  - Tense consistency
  - Dangling modifiers
  - Misplaced modifiers
- Have they used mixed metaphors?
- Are proper nouns spelled correctly?

A word after a word after a word is power.
—Margaret Atwood

How we critique

- **WE VALUE** the importance of not merely criticizing one another's writing but also being constructive. When we say something is wrong or could be better, we don't leave it at that.
- **WE SUGGEST** to the author how she could change her words to better encapsulate what she wants to say.
- **WE BRAINSTORM** as a group, leaving the writer to sift through our ideas and choose (or not) what works best for her.
- And importantly, **WE ENCOURAGE** one another and note exceptional sentences or phrasing, moments, descriptions, and details that we like.

It is nearly impossible to find every editing issue. Even the professionals miss things. For example, James Benn, author of Billy Boyle: A World War II Mystery Series, had this story to recount about a recent book:

After at least five read-throughs by nonprofessionals, I sent my book, *Solemn Graves*, on to my editor, who did a line edit. Three copyeditors read it. Three proofreaders read it. I reread it as I made the necessary revisions. Just prior to its release, a reviewer for *Goodreads* emailed me to say she'd found an error in the ARC (the Advance Reading Copy sent to bookstores and reviewers). Billy Boyle, my protagonist, had said this about a secondary character who has only one eye: "I watched his eyes dart back and forth . . ."

Really???

The Fixer-Upper

✓ **Practice editing for grammar**
✓ **Prep: Yes**

Purpose: This exercise is designed to give you practice editing.

Prep: Individual instructions prior to the group meeting:
1. Take a paragraph from a book or magazine article. Retype it exactly as is and don't change the order of the words, but:
    • Delete all punctuation
    • Change all capital letters to lowercase
    • Alter the spelling of basic words (their for there, to for too, etc.) that spellcheck won't pick up.
2. Make copies of your modified paragraph for group members.
3. Keep the original for yourself.

Materials for group: Each member brings copies of their modified paragraph.

Group instructions for the meeting: Edit each paragraph by properly punctuating, capitalizing, spell-checking, and otherwise making readable the paragraphs modified by the group members.
1. Determine an amount of time to be spent on editing each paragraph (ten minutes recommended).
    • One member hands out copies of their modified paragraph.
    • Other members edit with the intention of returning it to its original state.
    • The member whose paragraph it is reads the original version.
    • Discuss one another's editing and whether what they did to the passage worked or didn't work.
    • Repeat steps two through five for each group member.
2. This is harder than you think!

Critiquing Etiquette

✓ **Refine the art of critiquing**
✓ **Prep: No**

Purpose: This exercise is designed to help members learn how to critique a story and give productive feedback.

Materials for group: Poster board and marker

Group instructions for the meeting: Formulate a group plan on critiquing etiquette. Include both how to edit (what in particular to look for) and how to give feedback.

1. Choose one member to record responses on a poster board.
2. Each group member articulates what they want from having their work edited.
   - This could include but is not limited to:
     ○ Spell-checking
     ○ Grammar fixes
     ○ Sentence structure
     ○ Consistency
     ○ Timeline
     ○ Plot development
     ○ Commentary on voice
     ○ Format (e.g. footnotes, font, type, ease of readability)
   - As a group, decide which of the components will be included in the group editing process.
3. Discuss how members want to receive feedback.
   - Will comments be written on the work and given back to the author?
   - Will comments be given orally in group after the writer

reads their work?

- If comments are given orally, when will members make their observations?
  - During the reading?
  - Following the reading?

4. Discuss the way in which feedback is given (whether written or oral). What elements are important to your group? Remember, this is not about right or wrong, it is about what will work in your group. These may include but are not limited to:
   - Kindness (I may be wrong, but . . .)
   - Honesty (I think it would be stronger if you could . . .)
   - Having a balance between positive and critical (This is really good, but I wonder if . . .)
   - The sandwich critique: Starting with a positive, moving to a critique, ending with a positive (e.g. I like the way you use great action verbs and metaphor for what happens to Jake in this chapter. How about if you give the reader more detail on his motivation as to why he is doing what he is doing? But this chapter really is a page-turner.
   - Supportive (Have you considered trying this . . .)

5. Create a guideline for how members will edit and critique.

6. Before the next meeting, make copies of these guidelines to give to members.

7. At a future time, reevaluate periodically. How your group edits and critiques will evolve over time.

PART FOUR

From My Writing Group to Yours

In this final section of *All Write*, you will find:

- A special bonus chapter: Award-winning, national best-selling, and *The New York Times* Notable Book author Mette Harrison's Ten Step Novel Structure handout. Mette, who writes, among many other things, the Linda Wallheim series set in Mormon Utah, has graciously allowed us to share her technique which will help you plan, organize, or finesse your work in progress.
- Writing resources that we use.
- Examples of our writing from the books we are currently working on.
- And a conclusion that I hope is a beginning for you in your quest for a writing group to support and sustain you on your personal writing journey.

Writing this book has been a labor of love. Writing each of our own books is a labor of love. Will we find agents? Get published? Self-publish? Leave our manuscripts hibernating in Word? Who knows? It doesn't really matter. What matters is that we created this writing group, and we wrote. Whatever happens, we have enjoyed the process immensely. Now I want to encourage you to start or join a writing group so you can give the story in your head all you've got.

But one last word before I leave you.

Remember that your group comprises an assortment of people, all of whom have their own thoughts, beliefs, ideas, personalities, desires, expectations, dislikes, quirks, and strengths. The goal is to share and benefit not only from the similarities you may have, but also from the differences.

To work toward this common goal, the key element is communication. Establish a process for group discussion. Make it clear how members will bring up and discuss any issues that arise. And remember these key points:

Be respectful.
Listen without interruption.
Brainstorm ideas to get to a resolution. Be creative!

And if that doesn't work, it's okay to say, "Sorry, this isn't the right group for me." It's better to look for a right group than stay in the wrong group. Be proactive in taking care of yourself. You can create the right group for you. You deserve it! The moment is now.

In Gilda Radner's moving words:

I wanted a perfect ending. Now I've learned, the hard way, that some poems don't rhyme, and some stories don't have a clear beginning, middle, and end. Life is about not knowing, taking the moment and making the best of it, without knowing what's going to happen next. Delicious Ambiguity.

CHAPTER ELEVEN

Bonus—Ten Step Novel Structure by Mette Harrison

We endeavor to learn from people who have walked this path before us. Books and websites and blogs and workshops and classes are the stepping-stones on our writing journey. Along the way, we stop longer at some crossroads when we find the people, the techniques, or the resources that we connect with. I encountered Mette Harrison at book events and read several of her works. Impressed with her writing style and her résumé, I took an online writing course with Mette. Mette's structure for novel writing helped me organize my thoughts as I traversed my first attempt at penning a novel. As we do with everything we learn in our group, I shared Mette's teachings with the Shoreline Writers, and her technique resonated with the group. With Mette's permission, I am sharing her outline for writing a novel.

Ten Step Novel Structure, by Mette Harrison

1. Beginning

This is an introduction to the character and the world they live in to begin with. Think about how you're setting up both to change by the ending. Even if you have a rather slow start (which I am fond of), your main character must want/need something and be an active character, not a passive one, allowing other characters and events to act upon them. If you think *Star Wars*, remember Luke starts on Tatooine with his aunt and uncle, living an ordinary farming life. He complains (which is at least a kind of pushback) and says he wants to buy new droids.

2. Inciting Incident

This is the moment when things start to change. Sometimes this is in the first chapter, sometimes it's in the second chapter. It's what propels the rest of the story forward. In the first chapter, you may have a main character who wants something that turns out to be untenable, or that they quickly realize they don't want after all. The inciting incident must be part of the desire inside of them that will propel the rest of the plot forward, and the inner growth of the main character, as well. If we go back to *Star Wars*, the inciting incident is receiving the message from Princess Leia, which makes Luke go in search of Obi Wan (Ben Kenobi).

3. Resistance

A normal person is going to resist the inciting incident and the cascade of events that follow. They will try to back out of their participation, think of how they can get out of it, and backpedal. Some may try to go home. Others may try to be passive. Some might directly sabotage the action moving forward in hopes of not having to take risks—and not having to change. In *Star Wars*, this is when Luke realizes the danger in going with Han Solo.

4. Plan to Succeed

When at last the main character realizes that there's no way out and that, in fact, some part of them demands moving forward, the second half of the novel begins (though this may happen well before the second half in terms of page count). This is when we as readers strap in for the ride, and we expect to have lots of excitement, even if it's not all physical. For Luke, this is when he decides to commit to learning how to use the Force, and he's going onto the ship to rescue Leia.

5. Try and Fail Cycles

This may well be the longest section of your novel. Most of a novel is made up of failures, as it should be. Readers read because they want to be confirmed in their own belief that failure is a natural part of life and that they have to learn how to live through it. They also want to see other people humiliated and growing from setbacks, as they have to. The minimum for a novel is three try/fail cycles, but there can be far more than that. Remember as you're writing this section that the failures should not just be of one type. There can be defections from friends, fighting, deaths, injuries, learning that the magic doesn't work as expected, betrayals, and on and on. In *Star Wars*, this is when Han Solo and Luke are trying to rescue Leia.

6. New Obstacles

This is the section of the book where you introduce new problems that no one even considered possible before. It turns out the villain knows what they're doing and can stop them. The mentor is killed. Everything that was part of the previous plan goes out the window. There's a lot of havoc going on here, so don't cheat it in terms of page length. It's not going to be as long as part five, but it shouldn't be a single big problem either, rather a series of rising problems that make any solution impossible. In *Star Wars*, this is when Obi Wan is killed by Darth Vader.

7. Dark Night of the Soul

Once your main character realizes that all the effort of the last two parts is for naught and that there is nothing but failure and death waiting, this section is useful. You can't skip over this, but don't let it go on for too long because it can feel very depressing for the reader, and you don't want the main character to wallow. In *Star Wars*, this is when Luke and Han Solo are trying to destroy the Death Star, but there's no possible hope that it can happen.

8. Recommitment

This is the moment when the main character has to rely on themself to make things happen. No one else can intervene. There's no rescue from friends. It's the main character having to figure out what they have deep within that is going to win. It should be something that has been there all along, building, but wasn't the plan going in. In *Star Wars*, this is when Luke, despite the fact that there is no hope, decides to rely on the Force and try to take down the Death Star via the garbage chute.

9. Climax and Success

This is the highest moment of excitement in the story, the moment that everything else has been leading up to. But usually, this moment doesn't take long. It's what we've been aiming for, but once we're there, it turns out there are lots of other things to be done. In *Star Wars*, Luke destroys the Death Star and there's some hooting.

10. Denouement

It's important to show what happens after the climax because it helps to highlight the changes that have taken place from the beginning. Always look back to the beginning when you write the denouement, so you can touch again on some themes that were brought up there. In some ways, this may feel like a full circle moment, but it should also be a spiral, because it ends in a higher place than the beginning did, even if there's a return home. This is when Luke and Han Solo get their medals from Princess Leia and then everyone cheers. It's a triumphant, positive moment, but there should also be just a little sense of what things are left to be done. Even if you're not doing a sequel, the story should go on past this moment.

Ten Steps to Writing a Novel

✓ **Plotting the storyline**
✓ **Prep: Yes**

Purpose: This exercise is designed to help you lay out (in rough form) the forward movement of your novel, including your protagonist's challenges and hurdles, using Mette Harrison's "Ten Step Novel Structure." It will also orient the group to your writing style and the story line for your Work in Progress (WIP).

Prep: Instructions prior to the group meeting: Using Mette's Ten Steps, outline the plot for your book. You may not be able to answer all ten sections. Do your best.

1. Write your book outline using Mette's Ten Step Outline:
   i. **Beginning.** This is an introduction to the character and the world they live in. Describe how you're setting up both to change by the ending.
   ii. **Inciting Incident.** This is the moment when things start to change. Sometimes this is in the first chapter, sometimes it's in the second chapter. It's what propels the rest of the story forward.
   iii. **Resistance.** A normal person is going to resist the inciting incident and the cascade of events that follow.
   iv. **Plan to Succeed.** When at last the main character realizes that there's no way out and that, in fact, some part of them demands moving forward, the second half of the novel begins. This is when we as readers strap in for the ride, and we expect to have lots of excitement.
   v. **Try and Fail Cycles.** This may well be the longest section of your novel. Most of a novel is made up of failures, as it

should be.

vi. **New Obstacles.** This is the section of the book where you introduce new problems that no one even considered possible before.

vii. **Dark Night of the Soul.** Your main character realizes that all the effort of the last two parts is for naught and there is nothing but failure or death waiting.

viii. **Recommitment.** This is the moment when the main character has to rely on themself to make things happen.

ix. **Climax and Success.** This is the highest moment of excitement in the story, the moment that everything else has been leading up to.

x. **Denouement.** It's important to show what happens after the climax because it helps to highlight the changes that have taken place from the beginning.

2. Make hard copies of the plot outline for the group members.

Materials for group: Each member brings copies of their plot outline.

Group instructions for the meeting:
1. Each member reads aloud the plot outline of their story.
2. Questions and comments about the content follow.

ALL WRITE

✓ **Build a story incorporating the techniques that you have learned**
✓ **Prep: No**

Purpose: This exercise is designed to help you create a short story based on what you have learned in this book. It's for honing your writing skills and offering the group an opportunity to discuss the writing process.

Materials for group: One member brings a photograph to the meeting to be used as the backdrop for the story.

Group instructions for the meeting: Write a one- to two-page short story using the photograph as the setting. Utilize the various techniques you've learned for bringing depth and dimension to your writing. This is a three-part exercise.

1. **Part 1:** Reflect on the photo. Create a story. Write it down. Leave a few spaces between each written line. You will be adding more text later. (Allot twenty to thirty minutes for this.) Before you start to write decide on:
   - Point of View (POV)
     ○ First person (I, me)
     ○ Third person (he, she, they)
       » Third person limited (in one character's head)
       » Third person multiple (from several characters' perspectives)
       » Third person omniscient (the narrator knows everything)
     ○ What tense you will write in
       » Present
       » Past

- How many and who your characters will be (limit it to one, two, or at most, three).
- Write for the allotted amount of time, sketching out your story. Don't worry if you don't get it all down on paper but try to complete a rough draft. This is not meant to be a finished product, rather a first draft upon which to add the layers of the story.
- Everyone reads the draft of their story to the group.

2. **Part Two:** Add layers to further develop the story for your reader. (Allot twenty to thirty minutes for this.)
   - As presented by Rebecca Zanetti, layering includes, but is not limited to:
     - Dialogue
     - Action
     - Reactions
     - Emotions
     - The six senses (taste, touch, smell, sight, sound, feeling)
     - The setting (based on the picture)
     - Backstory
   - Techniques you've learned to help layering include:
     - The Camera Technique (Jeff Gerke)
       » As you work on the scenes in your story, ask yourself, "Can the camera see it?"
       » Have you put down on paper what you see in your imagination, so the reader can see it?
     - The Tip of the Iceberg (Hemingway)
       » Convey to the reader what your intentions are without spelling out every detail.
     - Metaphors and similes
       » One way to *show* in storytelling is to use metaphors and similes. Create one or two for your story.
       » Avoid clichés.
     - Psychic distance (John Gardner)

» Focus in, like a telescope, and narrow the distance between the narrator and the character and scene.

3. **Part Three:** Share your stories with the group followed by a group discussion. (Allot five to ten minutes per member for this, plus time for the group discussion.)
   - Each member reads their story aloud.
   - There are many iterations of how to add depth and dimension to a story. Members share how they approached this task.
   - Learn from one another so you will have more options when you write.

CHAPTER TWELVE
Our Writing

MARY REYNOLDS

Cockeyed

Why did I write this book?

My motivation to write came from an attitude of not "why?" but "why not?"

The week before my mother passed away, she'd sent me a birthday card asking me to write a story about her Texas kin. For as long as I can remember, she'd shared tales of her life growing up on a farm, a world that was opposite to my hardcore Yankee upbringing. Her request opened a door. I'd never considered becoming an author, but I figured what the heck. I'd been a painter all my life, so creating something from nothing wasn't new to me.

But the something from nothing wasn't entirely true. I'd spent time with my relatives in Texas—collecting eggs, milking cows, and jumping out of barn windows with toy guns while reenacting the Civil War.

Crafting the novel was easy. I wrote what I knew. I made my mother the protagonist and weaved the story around her life's narrative. The hard part was seeing I needed help polishing what I'd produced. Fortunately, I found a group of writers who wanted to join ranks and learn the craft in order realize their own dreams of becoming an author.

Sweet!

Cockeyed

Chapter One

———

REMEMBER WHOSE CHILD YOU ARE

Omaha, Nebraska – March 2000

I had no special talent for tending to the terminally ill, nor did I consider myself an overly compassionate being fit for such a serious job. My mother, Charlotte, had been sick on and off for quite a while and it was obvious the end was near. I took time off from my job in Connecticut and flew to her bedside in Omaha where she was living with my younger sister Annie. My older sister, Jeannette, and my youngest sister, Baby, had already come and said their final goodbyes.

I went there for her, but also for me, to see if Charlotte could give me one last thing before she walked through that door. I wanted to hear the words "I love you." See them fall from her lips. For her to mean it.

Charlotte was seventy-five years old and gravely ill. She never complained. If you met her on the street, you would not have guessed the clock was ticking on her. When I looked into her clear blue eyes, the beautiful eyes I remembered from childhood, her penetrating gaze could still make me confess to a crime I didn't commit.

Early in the week despite the monster that brewed within, Charlotte was ambulatory, cognizant, and high-spirited. I will also report that she was, as usual, obsessed with fashion. She dressed in lovely attire: skirts with ribbons and blouses with sequins even though it was noon. Every morning, I combed out her long grey hair and arranged it in a chignon just north of her neck.

"Mother, which of these hair combs would you like?"

"Oh, something with rhinestones, it makes me think of diamonds. Isn't it Friday?" she said.

"Could be—"

"What's the matter, Lizzy? Shouldn't you know? It's me who's sick, not you."

"Well, that's a matter of opinion," I said, as I set the comb in her hair.

I'm the first to admit I had a funny relationship with my mother. When talking to her directly I always called her Mother. Not Mom or Mommy. Those names seemed too intimate, too telling of an idealized love that movies—like *Terms of Endearment*—convince us to believe about the affection between a mother and daughter. Ours was not a typical relationship—Mother seemed more like an older sister to me, so behind her back, I took to calling her Charlotte. It just seemed to fit. Charlotte only heard me slip up once or twice and never seemed to mind. She always said I was her creative one, the one who was different. So the times I called her Charlotte, she laughed and chalked it up to the artist in me.

When doctors spewed information to my sisters and me about Charlotte's condition, the nurses scolded about the need to move her to a medical facility. Intestinal cancer seemed bad enough without sending her to the cold, cruel world of metal hospital beds, white cubicle curtains, and somber blue walls in her last days on earth. It was something we did not have the heart to do.

Every morning before Charlotte wiped sleep from her eyes, I dragged a chair to her bed and listened to her reminisce about her Texas childhood and her parents, May and Charlie Butler. She spoke of the good life she'd had with my father—not shedding a tear for the man who had departed five years earlier. Nor was there a word of criticism or disappointment about how things turned out or didn't turn out. If Charlotte were to err—it was on the side of accepting what was, and not what should have been. She found fault in little. Something I never understood.

As the week went on Charlotte become less interested in getting dressed, choosing instead to stay in her nightgown. She would only let me comb her hair.

Before I left her that Saturday afternoon in March, before I shut the glass doors to her bedroom, before I left her helpless to the Monster of Death who was closing in, she looked at me, pointed a finger, and whispered: "I did good in my life. I stopped a bad man from destroying a piece of paradise."

Bending closer, I said, "Mother, what are you talking about? What paradise?"

"Oh, something from long ago that nobody should have ever tried to mess with, because it would've been sinful to ruin land so sacred, so beautiful. I don't know what it is with most men. They're always trying to build things up or break things down. They can't leave well-enough alone."

"Mother, I don't understand a word you're saying. What men?" I asked, as I weighed whether she was drifting into delusional thinking.

"Don't be angry. There are things from my past I couldn't tell you."

"I'm not angry. Can you tell me now?" I asked.

"No, I promised never to mention what happened back in San Antonio. It's a secret."

"Are you sure it has to stay a secret?" I asked. I could see her blue eyes wandering like they used to when she'd talk about her parents. Something she was rarely willing to do.

She shook her head. "But that shouldn't stop you from finding out what happened, Lizzy. I trust you."

"Okay," I said, nodding my head as I swallowed her in a hug— one she did not, or could not return.

"Remember whose child you are," she whispered.

Growing up, Charlotte had given me an appreciation of her Texas ways. She'd wanted me and my sisters to remember her childhood stories and not forget our roots. Even though I could recite a bucketful of tales from her past, I hadn't been a witness to anything. As a journalist I know that facts drive stories. Without them narratives can be just fanciful poufs of the imagination. Adding a twang to the telling may delight listeners, but nonetheless, truth needs evidence. I'd never met my relatives. I'd never seen their photographs. And *hell*, I'd never even been to Texas.

With Charlotte's admission, a door swung open. I had to go to the Lone Star State and investigate her past to find out what was fact and what was fiction. Using tax records, I could locate her homestead in Victoria and then track down her family. There had to be someone still alive who could connect all the dots. If Charlotte had saved a piece of paradise, I had a right to know about it. She wasn't one to break a promise, but since I hadn't sworn any oaths the rule didn't apply to me.

Why did things have to be so difficult?

Why couldn't she tell me the secret?

Our hands met and held a solemn promise. Her smile faded as she melted into the mattress. The sparkling rhinestone clip she insisted on wearing every day was the only twinkle in the tangle of grey hair and white linen, that suggested she was the same fashion-clad woman from when I'd first arrived. With eyes closed, she fell away to a world that did not call my name. All along, I had fooled myself into thinking I'd known everything there was to know about Charlotte, but I was wrong—very wrong.

I departed with a silent goodbye and left her in the care of Annie. It was clear Charlotte wouldn't see another sunrise, something my fractured heart could not face. Her emotional coolness had never warmed my soul, but any starving person will tell you that cardboard tastes just fine, if it's all you have. At least that's what I'd believed in the past. But now the pain in my heart told me differently. Breaking news: Lizzy Lombardo Is Unlovable, There's No Hope, Even Lizzie's Mother Passes on Without Words of Affection.

Was it me or was it her?

Hours later, as I was disembarking from the plane in Hartford and walking to baggage claim, I flipped open my cell and called

Annie. "How's Charlotte?" I asked, keeping up my pace. Annie blurted out, "She's gone." And then began sobbing. My phone escaped from my fingers, crashed on the floor and slid out of view. Charlotte was gone. Everything went dark. I collapsed in a wave of passengers who danced around me.

"Are you all right? Do you need a doctor?" a kind voice said.

My face felt hot and flushed. "My mother's dead."

"I'm so sorry," a man said, as he escorted me to the safety of a chair. There was nothing else to be done.

Charlotte had left Texas at nineteen and never returned. She'd settled in New York for reasons she never said. I had chalked her relocation up to fate, never factoring in the oddity of her exile from the place she had been born. The place she had spoken of with such affection. The place that had shaped who she'd become.

When I had gone to stay with my mother in Omaha, the final week of her life, I was looking for love. Instead, she'd handed me a secret, and I had to figure out what to do with it.

Now, Charlotte was gone. But I had to find out what happened to her *then*.

CLAIRE SMITH

Georgiana: The Nearly Unrecorded but Full Life of Ella Georgiana Smith Cook

Why Did I Write This Book?

For years, an old boat sign reading *Georgiana* had been hanging on the porch of our old home. Our family knew she was an aunt who had lived four generations earlier, but no one knew much about her. So I set about trying to write a book about her for the family.

There were very few records about her, a fact that was true for most women of her time (1848-1930). I found I had to pry information from the documents of her male relatives and also make guesses based on what ordinary women's lives were like in her day and in her town. It felt like sculpting—taking a shapeless stone, chiseling it with each little point, and then watching a distinctive shape of a whole woman emerge.

Now, because of the interest and input and encouragement from Shoreline Writers, my book is becoming the story of a New England woman who lived through the Civil War, the advent of the railroad, the turn of the century, Prohibition, and the women's suffrage movement. The struggle now, instead of having no material, is having too much and figuring out what to carve away.

Georgiana:
The Nearly Unrecorded but Full Life
of Ella Georgiana Smith Cook

Her Full Share

Eventually, anyone who sits on our front porch spots the sign that reads Georgiana. It's a boat sign from an old wooden boat. Let's just say that the sign has character—it's over a hundred years old, and it looks it. But it's a hearty sign that sits quietly and securely above the inside porch door of this house that used to be a summer cottage and still acts like one. Sometimes I think the sign smiles down on the constant banging of the door beneath it.

After a bit of pondering, a newcomer asks: "Who is Georgiana?"

"She was the first Smith in our family to own this house. It was her summer cottage."

"How long ago was that?"

"Well, she and this house go back to 1882."

"And it stayed in the Smith family all these years?"

"Yup. It was the family summer cottage for generations of Smiths after her."

"Who was she? Do you know anything about her?"

"Well, we know she came from East Haddam. And we know her father was in the Civil War—"

That is when the curiosity and the questions, like heads watching a tennis match, snap away from Georgiana and turn to her father and the Civil War. Georgiana is then forgotten until the next first-time porch visitor.

When I married Peter Smith in 1985, I moved into Georgiana's Westbrook, Connecticut, cottage. Georgiana was his great-great-aunt, someone who died long before he was born. In 1972, Peter had purchased the cottage from Georgiana's estate, which had never been settled. By the time I moved in, he had turned it into a year-round home. At this writing, we've lived in it for over thirty-five years.

I walk in her rooms. I park my car in her horse barn. I rock on her porch. I hear the same tides lapping in and out. I look at the same Long Island Sound with the same islands. I see the same moonbeam streaming on the water at night, and the same sun rising faster than you would think possible over the horizon in the morning. And I see the same magical sun glitter on the water that for some reason appears each September.

I wonder if Georgiana is the spirit in the house who keeps it feeling like a summer cottage, which is not the color-coordinated ideal shown in catalogs, or the perfectly-worded, cozy, comfy, cuddly calm found in beach novels. But is the wonderful imperfection of wet towels with clashing colors hanging on anything that resembles a hook; Yankee and Red Sox baseball caps on rocking chair posts; forgotten drinks making rings on windowsills; sand on bathroom floors, sand around shower drains, sand mixed with chowder and ice on kitchen floors; little boy handprints on glass doors; friends' lost shoes; playing cards scattered on a table; and the sounds of pre-beach whines of impatient children, after-beach screeching of overtired children, and voices from one to ninety-one shouting over the too-loud music.

Over time, I became curious about Georgiana. Only a few drop-lets of facts about her had trickled down through the generations. Like nearly all women of her time, she was identified only by her relationship to the men in her life—she was the daughter of a Civil War soldier; she was the sister of a popular innkeeper; she was the local doctor's wife. Georgiana was born at a time when, with rare exceptions, only men fought the wars, had the professions, ran the businesses, owned the properties, made the laws, voted for the men who made the laws, and penned what was published. A time when only men had their stories recorded, and women did not.

Georgiana and I were born a century apart—exactly. She was born in 1849; I was born in 1949. Between her lifetime and mine, so much had changed, but yet so much had not. I began to wonder what she was like, what life was like for her, and if I could carve enough information out of century-old records to figure it out. As I began digging, I found a few official documents that bore her name. The family had a few photographs and a bit of ephemera. But as I tried to write her story, words like "probably," "likely," and "perhaps" became friends who overstayed their welcome. I "assumed," "presumed," and "guessed" my way through her story, learning that most of it had to be inferred from the news of her era and pried from the activities of the men in her life.

Then I found a newspaper article about her fifty-sixth wedding anniversary in 1924, when she was seventy-four. The article flattered her and her husband for their sociability and hospitality through the years. It listed her husband's lifetime achievements, which were many. For Georgiana, there was one sentence: she was "an ideal companion and homemaker, contributing her full share to the mutual happiness that has made married life worth living." Yes, it's a tad sexist. But it makes me wonder if her achievement is not life's greatest achievement, that of contributing your full share to happiness.

In writing Georgiana's story, I have tried to go beyond the flat presentation of the available facts to capture the essence of the woman who walked a hundred years ago under the same ceilings I do today. I have tried to capture the spirit of the woman who brought our family so much happiness. I have tried to capture her full share.

Brainy (in utero) Baby

Why did I write this book?

I wrote *Brainy (in utero) Baby* because no one else did. I first discovered approaches to increasing a baby's brain strength in utero over eighteen years ago when I was pregnant. Yet this information is still not common knowledge. And it should be.

At first, I felt uneasy about writing this book. Would people think I was obnoxious for focusing on brain strength and intelligence? And then I asked myself, if I were starting a family now, would I find this information valuable? Absolutely! I would gobble up every word and employ every strategy to boost my in utero baby's brain—after all, intelligence is rewarded.

With writing group encouragement and critiques from my first chapter to my last, I was able to complete my book—it was time to get published. A peek on Amazon reassured me there was a ready audience for books about how to increase a child's intelligence. And I was encouraged that I had a competitive advantage—my book promoted in utero brain boosting while other books focused on brain strengthening after the baby was born. My book was a first in its category—this was going to be easy!

I took an online class for help in writing a book proposal. I researched literary agents. I was ready. I confidently moved forward with query submissions and was immediately smacked with the requirement of a platform. Platform is the ability to market and sell a book because you are known and because you have influence. I am not known. I have no influence. I have no platform. I would not move forward. So I moved sideways!

I took a class about how to blog to build a platform. It offered tips about the differences between online writing and print-based writing as well as ways to optimize for search engines. My writing group continues to offer essential edits and encouragement for my new and evolving blog post writing style. I have a blog that is about to launch. My book is on hold until my blog builds a following, and I have a platform. See you online!

Brainy (in utero) Baby
BLOG POST

Exercise Builds In Utero Baby's Brain Strength

So, you're twenty squats deep and you're wondering, why does your in utero baby get smarter when you're the one doing the exercise?

When I was pregnant, my understanding was that the increased oxygen in my blood (from exercise) transferred to my wee one (through the umbilical cord), and THAT did the trick. Well, it's a factor, but it's only part of the equation. Turns out, there are a variety of reasons brain benefits are conferred upon in utero baby when enceinte mom is in motion.

Placenta Is Made Vigorous

- The placenta (an organ you create when pregnant) is made vigorous by regular exercise.

- The placenta attaches itself to the wall of the uterus to access maternal blood and via the umbilical cord, it provides oxygen, nutrients, and waste removal for in utero baby.

- "The placentas of women who exercise regularly throughout early and mid-pregnancy grow faster and function better than those of women who are healthy but don't exercise regularly. This means that, at any rate of uterine blood flow, **more oxygen and nutrients can get across to the baby of a woman who exercises** than to the baby of one who does not," according to James F. Clapp III, MD, author of *Exercising Through Pregnancy*.

Arouse Auditory and Vibratory Stimulation

- When you exercise, you are exposing in utero baby to a variety of sounds and movements.

- "Sound and vibratory stimuli before birth **may accelerate the development of the baby's brain**," according to Dr. Clapp.

Brain-Derived Neurotropic Factor

- Brain-Derived Neurotropic Factor, or BDNF for short (because that's a mouthful), is needed for learning and memory.

- When you exercise, your muscles secrete BDNF, which improves signal strength between neurons. Basically, **the more BDNF in the brain, the better the brain works**.

- A study at the University of Montreal led by Elise Labonte-LeMoyne, PhD **theorized that when pregnant mom exercises, the chemicals generated that are related to brain health transfer from the mother's bloodstream to baby's bloodstream**.

Epigenetics

- There is an epigenetic relationship between pregnant mom exercising and baby's brain health.

- Epigenetics is the study of gene expression, which is the process that makes a gene function. A gene must be expressed in order for its genetic trait to exert influence.

- Some inherited genetic traits can be **turned on or off like a switch**. Gene expression—the flipping of switches—is influenced by environment and lifestyle factors including exercise, diet, stress, environmental pollutants, drugs, tobacco, and alcohol.

- For in utero baby, **pregnant mom's exercise enthusiasm flips that switch to the strong brain position**. Michael F. Roizen, MD and Mehmet C. Oz, MD in their book *You, Having a Baby* maintain that **through epigenetics you can "influence some really important factors like your child's weight and intelligence."**

Bottom line: Exercise for pregnant women has a powerful and positive impact on the in utero baby brain. So, improve baby's brain (plus your bottom line) and crush another twenty squats!

Ponder the Importance of Building In Utero Baby's Brain Strength

Let's take a moment to use the brain to ponder the brain. A bit like introspection, only it isn't, but it kind of is.

While pretty much every organ in the body performs a dazzling feat of some sort,

- the **heart** drums 100,000 beats and pumps 2,000 gallons of blood a day,

- the newly discovered in 2018 organ called the **interstitium** (a squishy, fluid-filled, layered contraption) wraps around other organs to protect them (aww, so sweet!),

- the intricate vascular network (*organ system*, technically—but still dazzling) sloshes blood and lymph throughout the body for deliveries and pickups of oxygen, nutrients, and waste with FedEx efficiency, still . . .

only one organ stands (a head) above the rest: the brain.

Come to think of it, perhaps the brain's positioning is intentional—distinguishing itself with the requirement that we look up to it!

Maybe the body—organs, muscles, bones, and nerves—instinctively recognizes the nobility and magnificence of the brain because it knows the brain is in command. When the breath flutters with passion, the heart warms with love, or the nerves interpret tenderness, they can only do so because the brain is directing them to.

The magnificent brain also exerts influence—considerable influence.

In fact, **the brain influences every aspect of your life**, including your:

- Intelligence

- Memory
- Creativity
- Physical Health
- Degree of Happiness
- Ability to Feel Confident

All of these prominent human elements are contingent on the strength of your brain. Ponder that! And ponder the importance of strengthening these elements in your in utero baby's developing brain. What's more important than your baby's health, happiness, and cognitive abilities? No pondering is needed to know that's everything you'd want for your baby!

Make the brainy choice: Heed the magnificence of the brain and your "motherhood-as-a-higher-calling" instinct (and "fatherhood-as-a-higher-calling" instinct) and give your baby a gift that lasts a lifetime—a strong brain!

DEBORAH MANDEL

My Dead Body

Why did I write this book?

I've always wanted to write a novel. I've tried my hand at nonfiction and journal writing. I've taken numerous writing courses. But, when push came to shove, what could I write about? I'd settled on a subject—a therapist working with a Vietnam vet. I'm a psychotherapist with decades of experience working with trauma survivors, so it was in my wheelhouse. Write what you know.

Then something happened. I'd signed up for a writing class specifically with the intention of writing this book, when the instructor gave us an assignment: write a list of how many times you've experienced things in your life. For example, Dogs: five; Jobs: eight; pairs of shoes: twenty-two. In the middle of my list, I wrote this: number of dead bodies found: one. When I read my list aloud to the class, my teacher *told* me that's what I needed to write about.

I'd found a dead body on the beach when I was fifteen, and it had played a pivotal role in my early life. So I wrote the book. Rather it wrote itself. The first draft went quickly. The editing has taken much longer. I've put it away for long stretches of time. I've paid money to have it read by published authors and professional editors. Their feedback was helpful and confusing. I've started two other books in the meantime.

Will I finish this one? Will I finish it in a way that reflects me and not other peoples' input? I don't know. I hope so. Check back to find out how this story ends.

My Dead Body

CHAPTER 1

June 1, 1966

THE DAY I FIND A DEAD body starts out like every other day. I get up. I get dressed. I eat breakfast. I brush my teeth. And go to school. Today's the last exam of my sophomore year at The Oakes School—an all-girls private high school that I was sent to against my will freshman year.

After my dad disappeared from my life—a massive heart attack took him at age forty-three, when I was twelve—I'd gone from a straight A student in seventh grade to a straight C student in eighth grade. By the way, we're not allowed to use the word "dead" in describing my father. It's one of my mother's many bizarre quirks. She refers to him as being gone—as if he might come back.

My mother, not having a clue how to get me back on track academically, asked her then boyfriend—his name eludes me— for advice. She has the irritating habit of having someone else solve my problems. It used to be my father, which always worked out well for me, but now that he is no longer in the picture, it's whomever she's dating.

My fate was determined one night while I was cleaning up after dinner. Mom was sitting at the kitchen table talking to her latest paramour about me as if I weren't even there. I can still hear the whole conversation. "I'm at my wit's end . . . Hannah won't buckle down and do her homework . . . her grades are terrible . . . it's such a poor reflection on me as a mother . . . Blah . . . Blah . . . Blah." Okay, so I don't remember their exact words, but you get the drift. It was Mr. Fill-in-the Blank's opinion that I should go to the private school his daughter attended.

It took my mother about five seconds to agree with his assessment of my failings, all due to my being in the wrong school—public, not private—and before week's end, I had an appointment with the headmistress for an admissions interview. I didn't want to go to another new school where I wouldn't know anyone except Mr. Know-It-All's daughter, Little-Miss-Know-It-All, whom I didn't even like.

It was bad enough I'd been uprooted in seventh grade because we'd moved to a new town and then had been derailed by my father's passing three months later. I *had* to stay in public school with my friends. There *had* to be a way.

I made a calculated attempt in my interview with Miss Beckett, the headmistress, to convince her that she wouldn't want me in her prestigious school. But at the end of the hour, after informing me I was not the caliber of student she normally accepted, Miss Bucket, as she was referred to by my friends anyway, took me on as a personal challenge. And the icing on the cake—I get a need-based scholarship, which means I'm assigned to work in the kitchen during lunch period three days a week, waiting on my schoolmates.

So here I am, last day of school, sitting in homeroom and watching the clock. As soon as the dismissal bell rings, my best friend Pab and I leave for her house. We head downstairs to the rec room, where Pab suggests we have something to drink. I'm excited because I think she means soda, which is *verboten* in my home (that's a German word meaning absolutely forbidden, like Jews were in Germany during the war, and which, by the way,

I am. Jewish, not German). It's another quirk of my mother's—
NO SUGARY FOODS ALLOWED!

But Pab has something entirely different in mind.

"My dad makes these cocktails," she says. "Screwdrivers. Want one?"

Hmmm. It doesn't take me long to decide. "Why not?" I say. I'm almost sixteen, and I've practically raised myself and my siblings since my dad passed and my mom went off the deep end. I'm ready for a liquid taste of the adult world.

I flop down on one of the oversized, fringed pillows on the floor. The room is in the lower level of their cedar-shingled house on Ocean Avenue, where there are three identical houses in a row. Hers is the middle one. A large magnolia tree, in full bloom, sets it apart from the other houses. Mrs. Buckley loves to garden, and their yard is the nicest around. My yard has nothing in it. Since my dad rode off into the sunset a mere eighty-six days after we moved in, the house wasn't even finished. He and my mother were doing all the finish work themselves, like walls and ceilings and floors, never mind landscaping. Our yard looks like an abandoned field where someone threw some grass seeds and hoped for the best.

It's a beautiful spring day, and the sun is streaming in through the sliding glass doors that lead out to the backyard. It shines through cut crystal glasses that are stacked at the far end of the wooden bar, sending prisms of light dancing around the room. It reminds me of the crystal I have hanging in my bedroom window. Every morning, when the sun hits it, my room fills with hundreds of rainbows. A blast of color in my otherwise completely dreary world.

As Pab goes behind the bar, a cascade of rainbows shimmers across her face. She's pretty. Long brown bangs hang over her blue eyes, and her thick hair reaches halfway down her back. She has the cutest nose, kind of turned up. The opposite of mine. I have a classic Jewish *schnozz*. That's the Yiddish word for "beak," which is how Jewish noses are often described. It's not the biggest hooked nose in my family, but definitely noticeable.

Pab chooses two of the taller glasses. Yikes! Watching how confidently she makes our drinks, I'm sure it isn't her first time.

The room has a cracked and worn brown leather couch, a nubby orange La-Z-Boy recliner, and a color TV. It's the kind of room that's fun to hang out in. There are ashtrays on the bar and coffee table, and several open packs of Lucky Strikes lying around. The Buckleys all smoke, including Pab, who smokes with her parents. Most of my friends' parents smoke, but they'd kill their kids if they ever caught them with a cigarette. But Pab doesn't have to sneak. Her parents are cool like that.

"What do ya think of the drink?" Pab asks after I've taken a few sips, then a few larger gulps.

"I like it. Tastes like orange juice. What else is in it?" I ask.

"Just OJ and vodka. And the best part is that vodka doesn't smell like most booze does, so no one will know we've been drinking."

She has this all figured out.

"Cool," I say, and in a short time finish off the rest of my vitamin C-fortified drink.

"Want to walk to the beach?" Pab asks when we're both finished.

I feel much happier now than I did when I first got here.

"Yeah," I say, suppressing a giggle.

"Just gonna have a cigarette, then we'll go. My parents don't want me smoking out on the street. They say it looks trashy!"

"Your parents are too funny, Pab. So as long as you stay inside you can do whatever you want? Just don't look bad to the neighbors?"

"Yep," she says with a chuckle, lighting up.

She stubs out her butt in an overflowing ashtray, and we head outside. The world looks clean and crisp. If this is what drinking is all about, I'm all about drinking. My brain is on fire. I'm revved up and ready to go. The green grass and blue sky vibrate with color, like I'm seeing them for the first time.

We walk down to Pequot Avenue, then along the beach at the water's edge. I'm careful not to get my feet wet. It's way too cold.

Pab doesn't seem to care and the waves wash over her small feet with their pink nail polish and matching flip flops. I'm envious of her feet, too. Mine are huge. Size 9.5.

I'm mesmerized by the way everything looks today. The sand glimmers with tiny crystals of quartz, and the water shimmers in the sunlight. I'm at the beach. I'm with my best friend. School is over. Summer is here. Nothing could possibly spoil this perfect day.

Seaweed has washed up along the shoreline, along with a few beat-up lobster pots, empty soda cans, and a smelly, half-eaten fish. All the normal beach junk. Further down the beach, a shape stands out, stranded in the middle of the sand.

"What is *that*?" I say, eying the unusual shape.

"Don't have a clue. Let's check it out," Pab says.

"It's probably just a really big piece of driftwood," I say.

"Sure," Pab says, sounding not so sure.

As we get closer, reality sets in. I blink a few times, trying to clear my vision, afraid it is being clouded by the alcohol I've drunk. This is not a big piece of driftwood. It's not a pile of seaweed. It's not some part of a smashed boat. It's a man. A dead man. A long-dead dead man. Laying face up and spread-eagle in the sand. Missing a foot. His bloated face and hands blackened in his watery grave. A bulging belly with a shiny metal belt buckle with the engraved letters JCW cinched tightly across it.

I look again. And I look again, my brain trying to make sense of what I'm seeing. What is a dead man doing on the beach? What are we supposed to do? Should we look for ID in his pockets? My heart races.

"Pab," I say, "could the vodka cause us to hallucinate?" Seriously, I've never had a drink before, so I don't know.

She shakes her head. "No—the body is real. Shit."

"What should we do? This is crazy," I say. My brain is no longer operating on warp speed. It's moving in slow motion now. Like, really slow.

"Yeah it is. Beyond crazy. I wonder how it even got here. It's way up higher than the tide line," Pab says, inching a little closer and bending over the distorted form.

"There was a storm a few days ago. Maybe it got washed up then, and no one's seen it. We have to call for help," I say. My euphoria has dissolved, and I've catapulted from feeling on top of the world back into the quicksand that held me captive for so long after my father left. It settles in my chest, threatening to drown me internally.

"Yeah, guess so. Sure wish I had a cig," Pab says.

It's always so simple for Pab.

On the short walk between the disfigured and decomposing body and the nearest house, we double back several times to make sure the one-footed corpse is still there. Each time part of me hopes it won't be. But that would be plain crazy.

We walk up the curving stone walkway of the first house we come to. It's more like a mansion. Hesitantly, I take the four steps up to the front porch, then knock on the oversized solid wood door, tentatively at first, then more insistently. Finally, an older woman opens the door and glares at us. She looks at least fifty and is dressed in a two-piece beige pantsuit with a maroon silk scarf, a string of pearls around her neck, and a huge pearl in each ear. She's even wearing pumps. No one's mother I know dresses like that during the middle of the day. Plus, it is almost summer for God's sake.

"I'm sorry to bother you, Ma'am, but may we please make a phone call?" I say, using my best Oakes School manners. "We just found a dead body on the beach, and we need to call the cops."

It isn't hard to tell by the look on her face that she does not believe me. So I turn up the charm. Learned this at The Oakes too. "Really Ma'am, there is a dead man on the beach across the street. We have to tell the police."

"What are you talking about?" she asks. "Do you expect me to believe that there is a body on *my* beach?" *Her* beach?

"Yes, Ma'am, there really is a dead body on *your* beach," I say. "So please let us use your phone to call the police so they can take care of it." My voice is rising, and I don't care.

After what feels like ten minutes of this, she relents. "Very well then. You may use my phone but go around to the back of the house to the *Service Entrance*. I'll meet you there."

Pab and I look at each other. I can tell by the scowl on her face that she is as annoyed by this woman as I am.

"Who does she think she is?" Pab asks in a hushed voice as we walk down the driveway to the rear of the house.

"Really," I say.

Worst thing—that woman isn't done with her disdainful-annoying-rich-bitch attitude. She opens the back door but blocks our entry.

"I will allow you girls to use my phone, but under no circumstances are you to give the police my address," she says. "Do. You. Understand?" Each word enunciated and punctuated for effect.

"Jesus," I mutter under my breath. And yes, even good Jews use that expression.

"But if we can't tell them where we are, how do we tell them where the body is?" Pab asks.

"I will not be party to a teenage prank; therefore, you may not use my address."

"What do you suggest we tell them then?" Pab asks, with no hint of polite society manners.

"Give them a general idea of where you are, then go outside and wait."

With that, she moves aside and beckons us into a small room containing a table with a phone, one straight-backed cane chair, an umbrella stand, and a coat rack. Two large oil paintings of hunting scenes hang on the wall. Galoshes sit by the door.

Pab gestures for me to make the call. I look up the number in the directory by the phone. "Officer," I say when someone finally answers, "my friend and I just found a dead body." Took him long enough to pick up the phone. If I were being murdered, I'd be dead.

"I can't tell you where I am exactly," I say, in answer to his very predictable question about the whereabouts of the body.

"Yes sir, I am telling you the truth."

"Yes sir. There is really a dead body. It's on Pequot Avenue, on the beach just past the lighthouse."

As I describe our find to the officer on the other end of the phone line, I am lectured about teenagers wasting police time and resources. After several minutes of preaching about the trouble with the youth of today, the officer tells me they'll send someone to check our story.

"It's mandatory," he says.

I hang up the phone. My hands are shaking, and my breath is coming in short, raspy gasps. The police are coming, and they are going to know I've been drinking. I'll be grounded for the rest of the summer. Great.

Pab and I head out the door to wait by the beach. I look across the sand, and the image of the bloated, footless corpse floods my mind. My stomach heaves. I puke. It's orange.

CHAPTER THIRTEEN
And by the way...

...everything in life is writable about if you have the outgoing guts to do it, and the imagination to improvise. The worst enemy to creativity is self-doubt.
—Sylvia Plath

I hope you have found this book useful as you establish a new writing group or revamp an existing one. I would appreciate any feedback about what you found helpful or even downright ridiculous. Please send all communications to Deborah Mandel @ debbielmandel@gmail.com.

I wish you all-out, bodacious, unparalleled, profound, and unconditional success with your writing group as well as your work in progress. Whether you are writing for the love of writing or writing or to sell your book and make the *New York Times* Bestseller List, enjoy the process. Each word is a gift. Each sentence a gift. Each paragraph a gift. And that moment when you type the end is the ultimate gift to yourself and to whoever is fortunate enough to read your story.

CHAPTER FOURTEEN
Writing Resources

Books

- *Dreyer's English: An Utterly Correct Guide to Clarity and Style*, by Benjamin Dreyer
- *Eats, Shoots & Leaves: The Zero Tolerance Approach to Punctuation*, by Lynne Truss
- *Garner's Modern English Usage*, by Bryan A. Garner
- *Mastering the Craft of Writing: How to Write with Clarity, Emphasis and Style*, by Stephen Wilbers
- *On Writing: A Memoir of the Craft*, Stephen King
- *Reading like a Writer: A Guide for People Who Love Books and for Those Who Want to Write Them*, by Francine Prose
- *Spellbinding Sentences: A Writer's Guide to Achieving Excellence and Captivating Readers*, by Barbara Baig
- *Spunk and Bite: A Writers Guide to Bold, Contemporary Style*, by Arthur Plotnik
- *The Chicago Manual of Style, Seventeenth Edition*
- *The Elements of Style*, by William Strunk and E. B. White
- *The Emotions Thesaurus: A Writer's Guide To Character Expression*, by Angela Ackerman and Becca Puglisi
- *The Everything Guide to Writing Your First Novel*, by Hallie Ephron
- *The First 50 Pages*, by Jeff Gerke
- *The Seven Basic Plots: Why We Tell Stories*, by Christopher Booker
- *The Writer's Idea Book: Fiction, Nonfiction and Screenplays*, by Jack Heffron
- *The Writing & Critique Group Survival Guide: How to Give and Receive Feedback, Self-Edit, and Make Revisions, by Becky Levine*
- *Thirteen Ways of Looking at the Novel*, by Jane Smiley
- *Wired for Story: A Writer's Guide to Using Brain Science to Hook Readers from the Very First Sentence*, by Lisa Cron
- *Writing and Selling Your Mystery Novel*, by Hallie Ephron
- *You've Got a Book in You: A Stress-Free Guide to Writing the Book of Your Dreams*, by Elizabeth Sims

Online Resources

Research your topics online. There are numerous online resources covering everything from how to come up with ideas to write about, how to write down these ideas to create a book, how to edit your book, and, finally, how to get your book published. I could not begin to do justice to them here and would certainly leave out some we have found valuable. The one tip I will leave you with to help you navigate the online universe is to try the search engine Soovle, which is a customizable engine that unites the suggestion services from all the major providers in one place.

Classes

Enroll in writing classes. Don't miss the writing opportunities presented through local educational facilities. See which universities and colleges offer Adult Ed courses. Is there a Lifelong Learning Organization near you? Check your community's Adult Ed schedule for writing classes. Any writing course you take is a step in the right direction. And you might meet your future writing group mates there!

Conferences

Attend writing conferences. They are great resources for learning the art of writing as well as for meeting established authors, agents, publishers, and fledgling writers like yourself. Look for conferences focused on your particular genre.

Made in the USA
Middletown, DE
30 May 2021